CW00765541

Surfing
the
Edge

**A Survivor's Guide To
Bipolar Disorder**

by
Adam Dickson
Faye Trickett
Alastair Donald

with
Chris Kelly
RMN Dip. H/E M.A.

Surfing The Edge
A Survivor's Guide To Bipolar Disorder
Copyright ©2015 Adam Dickson

British Library Cataloguing in Publication Data.
A catalogue record for this book is available from the British Library.

ISBN: 978-0-9934776-0-7

Castra publishing

About the Author

Adam Dickson is a novelist and screenwriter. His novels are *The Butterfly Collector* (2012), *Drowning by Numbers* (2014), *Billy Riley* (2020), *Indigo Blue* (2022) and also *A Waltz Through The Dark Wood* (2023) a collection of short stories. He has also co-written three non-fiction books in the sports genre, and a book on mental health, *Surfing the Edge: a survivor's guide to bipolar disorder.*

His screenplays include adaptations of both novels, and a pilot for TV. In February 2020, he appeared as an expert in the CBS Reality crime series *Murder by the Sea*. The episode titled *Neville Heath, the Lady Killer* documents the real-life case of ex-RAF pilot Neville Heath, who was hanged at Pentonville Prison in 1946.

www.adamdickson.co.uk

Contents

Acknowledgements

Thanks to the following for their contributions to this book, and for their unfailing support and enthusiasm over the long haul leading up to publication:

Liz Gordon, Brilliant Fish PR & Marketing for editing. Annabel Sampson for proofreading. Professor Geoff Searle for his kind comments and suggestions regarding the video. Susan England for critique and encouragement. Wessex Writers for critique of early drafts and a professional appraisal. Alex Dickson for formatting and for his iconic cover design.

A special thanks to the authors' families and friends who shall remain nameless, but without whose love and support none of this would have been possible.

Introduction

Manic depression has been around a long time. The first case was recorded in 1st Century Greece. Some of our most influential writers and artists have suffered its extremes, along with countless thousands of ordinary people throughout the ages. The disorder can affect anyone. For those of us living with the illness, the experiences are memorable: balanced on a high wire without a safety net, or plunged into a trough of black despair. The middle ground comes as a welcome relief, respite from a storm that ravages lives and leaves a permanent shadow.

This book comes from a series of conversations – shared experience on the delicate subject of mental illness and its often catastrophic effect upon the individual. The authors come from markedly different backgrounds in terms of education and environment, but face the same challenges in their struggle to come to terms with this complex illness.

The question and answer format is easy to follow: the chapters cover the formative years from childhood to adolescence and into adulthood, exploring symptoms at different stages of development. Told with honesty and humour, *Surfing the Edge* takes the reader on a dramatic, sometimes disturbing journey into mental illness.

The light at the end of the tunnel can be seen in terms of survival. Fellow sufferers can take courage from the message of hope within these pages, that a full and productive life can be lived in spite of such an apparent disability. The final chapter, 'Coping Strategies', offers practical advice on living with manic depression and looks at the options from a holistic point of view.

It is the authors' sincere wish that this book will both educate and inform, and lead the reader to a better understanding of the illness in general.

We have used the original term manic-depression frequently throughout the text, as well as its more modern counterpart, bipolar disorder. The original term, we feel, needs no further explanation and paints a suitably graphic picture of the illness. This should in no way detract from the primary aim of the book – to inform the reader.

Adam Dickson

Introduction by Chris Kelly

As a mental health professional, I have worked with people diagnosed with bipolar disorder for over twenty years. While I don't claim a special understanding or comprehensive knowledge because of this fact, I have gained a valuable insight into the illness and how it impacts people's lives on a daily basis. Those I have been fortunate enough to work with have always impressed upon me their resilience and a far greater capacity to manage their problems than many of the services designed to help them.

Bipolar disorder (formerly known as manic depression) is a vast subject area; there are countless journal articles, medical books and websites devoted to it. You only have to tap 'bipolar disorder' into Google to find a selection of about 1500 texts on the subject. These will range from text books, academic studies, as well as collections of books that offer a variety of general mental illness and bipolar experiences. Without some guidance or advice it can be very difficult to choose a text that will inform and assist you in understanding more about this vast area.

However, for a clear understanding of its impact upon the individual and those closest to them, a more direct experience is necessary. As a lecturer in Mental Health Nursing at Bournemouth University, I would often invite service users in to share their experiences with the students. I could observe the profound effect on the students' understanding of the illness and how the sessions better prepared them in their training to become health professionals. Their evaluations were always positive and the learning delivered in such a dynamic way that it added to their experience – but no longer from someone they had only ever seen as a service user or patient. We learn so much more, and on different levels, from those who have experienced the very problems we are called upon to help.

My initial motivation for contributing to this book

stems from this firm belief.

As a practicing community mental health nurse I am continually learning from service users and their families about how to live with bipolar disorder. By working alongside those who experience it for themselves, we, the healthcare providers, are constantly learning about the illness and how best to treat it. I believe this book will help a range of people, whether a service user, family member or health professional.

Surfing the Edge is the shared experience of three people who live with the illness. The text covers history, diagnosis and treatment, as well as personal accounts on many related subjects and their effect on the sufferer, the family, and those who work with them. The personal testimonies of Faye, Adam and Alastair will increase your understanding of the illness and, hopefully, stimulate further discussion. By increasing the general knowledge and understanding of bipolar disorder, better coping strategies can be found that will work on a long-term basis.

The book gives an unsparing account as to the nature of the illness and how it may be accommodated in people's lives. Psychologist Patricia Deegan outlined her own experience as both a health professional and a service user:

> *'Those of us who have been diagnosed are not objects to be acted upon. We are fully human subjects who can act and in acting, change our situation. We are human beings and can speak for ourselves.'*

It is my sincere hope that this book provides insight and information on a subject that has been so widely debated over the past few decades. Bipolar disorder drains the energy, saps the motivation and weakens the resolve of those affected by it. And yet, for many people, having the illness has somehow enriched their lives. Perhaps it is – as Alastair refers to it –'both a curse and a blessing too'.

For anyone with mental illness, having someone around you with a genuine desire to help, whose experience is backed-up with wisdom and compassion, is essential to recovery. I'm sure the testimonies in this book will help prove that, in spite of the difficulties encountered, a full and productive life can be lived by those effected, and that we each have a role to play in making this happen.

Childhood

'At night, I would lie awake, listening to the silence, convinced I was alone.'

1. Looking back, were there any factors in your childhood that might have played a part in your later diagnosis?

Alastair: Firstly, I would say that I had a happy childhood. My father was in the R. A. F. We moved around quite a lot and so I didn't feel as if I had any roots. Because of that, I believe I learned how to make friends quickly. Whether this was a survival technique or a natural part of my character, I don't know. Perhaps it was a mixture of both. Whatever the reason, I seemed to have no real problems fitting in.

So, I would have to say, no, there was nothing in my childhood that led me to believe that I would have mental health issues later on in life.

I can remember living in Cyprus, which I loved. I've got two older sisters and they went to boarding school around the ages of twelve, thirteen. I was at school in Cyprus, on the RAF base, which I also enjoyed. But then my parents wanted me to go to public school back in England, which actually meant prep school. I had no desire to do this at all. In fact, I found the whole idea quite daunting. My parents would continue to live in Cyprus and I would be sent off abroad at the age of ten. A dreadful business, as far as I was concerned.

Faye: How did that make you feel?

Distraught. Abandoned. A lot of this was due to the fact that I wouldn't get to see my parents at weekends as they were so far away. I came from a close and stable family background and the thought of leaving it really upset me. And when I finally said goodbye to my mum, here I was in this strange environment. I didn't know anyone. The other boys were complete strangers to me. All I knew was that I wasn't going to see my parents for three months. And three months for a child of ten seemed like a very long time indeed.

Adam: Did you manage to adapt?

The first month, I hated it. I had to get used to a completely different regime than the one I'd been used to, with boys I'd never met before.

But I also had another major problem that I found equally distressing. I used to wet the bed. Now this was a boarding school, remember. I slept in a dormitory with about sixteen other boys and this would happen, perhaps not every night, but certainly every other night. I would lie there awake, in my sodden pyjamas and sodden sheets, ashamed, afraid I would be found out. Some of the boys did find out and I was teased mercilessly.

This issue prevented me from being involved in the pillow fights that went on and made me avoid contact with other boys in the dormitory. It really did have a huge effect on me. The whole thing was extremely embarrassing and made me dread the night times in the dormitory.

Faye: God, that must have been awful for you. But I can relate to that feeling of separation so much. My dad was in the Navy, and he was away a lot. I was very much a daddy's girl and missed him terribly when he was away. That was always a source of sadness for me back then.

My brother was born when I was five and, suddenly, instead of it just being me and my mum, it was me and my brother. I felt totally pushed out by that. You know – she didn't want me any more because she was too busy with him.

One time, I'd just started school. We'd moved house, and I didn't know my way home. No-one came to pick me up, so I ended up following the lollipop lady home. I don't know why Mum didn't pick me up; it was just one of those things. But it did have a profound effect on me. It felt like I didn't matter, that I was insignificant in some way.

Alastair: Do you see this as a catalyst for your problems later on?

Not particularly. It's just an early childhood memory that sticks in my mind. Perhaps I was naturally fearful, or extra sensitive, I don't know. Or, maybe it's just that fear everyone has of being abandoned, of being left on your own.

Adam: My memories of childhood aren't all that clear. I can recall summer holidays at my grandmother's, which I loved, but not much else. The house was detached and set in its own grounds at the end of a long country lane. The neighbours had a swimming pool that my cousin and I could use occasionally. I certainly enjoyed the isolation. I didn't mix with many children my own age, and being alone seemed to suit my personality.

Most of the time, I lived in my imagination. I loved cowboy films and would re-enact violent scenes in the garden, with my cousin as sidekick. I loved television, films in particular, and would scan the Radio and TV Times looking for suitable, or unsuitable material.

I've often wondered where my fascination with violence came from, considering how passive I was as a child. I wasn't keen on sports and had no physical outlet. I used to sit and draw for hours, or study history books with graphic depictions of battle scenes and bloody executions.

Alastair: How did the isolation affect your schooling?

I suppose it's similar to Faye's experience in a way. I remember my first day at school and my mum leaving me in the playground. The feeling of being abandoned. That same feeling of being alone then became a regular feature of my childhood. Laying awake at night, listening to the silence, convinced I was alone in the house. All pretty common stuff for a child, I suppose, but I do remember being fearful a lot of the time.

Faye: In ways that would affect your mental state later on?

I'm always looking for connections between my childhood and my future mental state. I believe that no single event caused the illness that crippled me later. But my personality certainly predisposed me to mood swings and periods of isolation. I was the classic introvert, much happier in my room, listening to music or reading a book.

Paradoxically though, I did have friends and enjoyed the usual boys stuff like climbing trees and running through peoples gardens! Things like hospitalisation and major psychosis were a long way off, but there were causes for concern even back then.

2. Did you enjoy normal childhood activities and did you mix well with other children?

Alastair: Well, I did, but my behaviour was almost a double-edged sword. Because of the bed-wetting and boys taking the piss out of me – if you'll pardon the pun – I became the joker. I was the one who made people laugh. From the age of ten, eleven, I just mucked around. Because of this, I became quite popular, and was seen as the school fool.

As one of the older boys at prep school, before you did your common entrance, you were given some responsibility. You might be made a monitor, perhaps, and the younger children would have to listen to you. I was never given this privilege. I was always seen (and this followed me right through public school) as being very immature. It was almost 'Don't give Alastair any responsibility because he's the school joker!'

But, somehow, I did pass my common entrance to go to public school – to the absolute astonishment of my Headmaster, who thought I had no chance whatsoever. After all, I was the one who'd fart at the back of the classroom and get the peashooter out – the one who never paid attention in lessons. My more outrageous tendencies were in force even then. But that's what happened. I passed my common entrance and went to a place called Epsom College.

Adam: You had no academic ambitions at all at the time?

None whatsoever! I really didn't. I treated it all as a bit of a joke, something I had to put up with because I had no choice. But of course, it was expected that at some point, I would knuckle down and make the grade. The school fees were an incentive in themselves. And, of course, my parents were hoping for a sign that I would change my foolish behaviour and start studying. Which I didn't.

That's it, really. So began my career as the laziest man on the planet!

Faye: I was different in that respect. I threw myself into studying as a means of escaping what was going on around me. From the age of about seven, I was bullied. Just because I was a little bit different, I suppose. Eventually, I had to change schools.

Looking back, I didn't have a particularly happy childhood. I've always been a loner. I did try to mix with other children but found it really difficult. I went to Brownies when I was seven, and did that for a few years. But, I never really enjoyed being around other kids. Playing football or netball, or whatever it was they were playing. I felt the whole thing was beyond me.

Alastair: Any pranks and naughtiness, wilful behaviour?

Not really, sorry to disappoint you, Alastair! I just threw myself into my schoolwork, especially when I changed schools. And I found that, actually, I was quite bright. So that became my thing. Faye – the school swot. The intelligent one. That persona stayed with me throughout my teenage years.

My dad's coming and going was a big thing. When it was just me and him, I was happy. He made such a fuss of me. Later on, when I was a teenager, he developed depression and that was very difficult to deal with. In fact, it blew our entire family apart. The house was like a war zone. What with my hormones, my dad's depression, and my mum trying to hold it all together, it was absolute hell.

Although he's never said anything, my brother must have found it really hard to deal with as well. But he's turned out all right. He's got no depression or anything.

Adam: I always thought I had an abnormal childhood, until I listened to other people's stories. I now believe mine was privileged. My dad worked hard to provide for us and always made sure we went on holiday regularly. We'd all go off in a camper van to places like Scotland and the Lake District. I remember catching a huge crab in St Peter Port, Guernsey, and climbing in World War Two gun emplacements. My dad was quite a character. He had a wide circle of friends and unlike me, was totally at ease in social situations.

The important thing for me was that I was never denied anything. I went swimming, cycling, Saturday morning cinema, all that stuff. Christmas was most memorable. The whole family stayed at my grandmother's for a week. I can still walk through the rooms of that house in my mind now and remember every detail, even though it was knocked down many years ago. I loved being there. So, yes, I've got good memories of my early family life in general.

Faye: How did you get on with other children?

Although I had friends right the way through school, and appeared to make friends easily, I was often withdrawn. Right from an early age, I felt the need for some kind of mask. I was a highly sensitive child. Very creative. At some of the schools I went to, this wasn't a trait to be proud of. Boys were regarded more for their fighting abilities than their talents for the arts, and you were soon made aware of this. I felt the need to protect myself at all times. Other children were a threat in some way, a constant source of worry.

Like Alastair, I had no ambition. Whatever talents I had were stifled by an inner anxiety and the fear that I was somehow different from my peers. I was usually too busy obsessing over girls and avoiding the playground scuffles to concentrate on schoolwork. Apart from English and Art, which I had a natural talent for, I don't recall any serious interest in any of the lessons.

It's hard to be objective about early childhood. There are so many blanks and vague recollections that the whole thing is a blur. In many ways it's as if I wasn't there at all. Certain things stand out vividly, like the details of my grandmother's house and playing cowboys and Indians in the garden with my cousin. But apart from that, there isn't all that much I remember.

'I remember my first day at school and my mum leaving me in the playground. The feeling of being abandoned.'

3. Do you have any hereditary basis for your diagnosis?

Alastair: I don't believe so, in my case. Although my grandmother, who I never met, did die in unusual circumstances. This was never talked about in my family, but I believe she committed suicide. I don't actually know this for a fact, but this was the impression I got from the few details that came out later. She was in her fifties, I believe, and my mum loved her very much. Beyond that, I can't say. Certain subjects were taboo in my family and that, I suppose, was one of them.

Was she suffering from depression at the time? I don't know. And if so, would her suicide – if it was that – shed some light on my later mental health problems? Again, I don't know. But I don't believe, genetically, that there has been anyone else in my family who has suffered manic depression.

Faye: For me, the obvious answer is yes. Dad had always been prone to depression, although he's not bipolar. He's been well now for about fifteen years, but there's always that underlying tendency towards depression. He did get very ill with a ruptured aortic aneurysm last year and nearly died. Weeks spent on an intensive care unit took its toll and he got very down at that point. It took him a long time to build himself back up again.

My grandparents died quite young, so I don't have a record of there being any sort of history with them. As far as I know, there's no-one on my dad's side that suffers mental illness.

Adam: Well, I can say, without any doubt, that there is a strong genetic link in my family. Certainly on my mother's side. Two of my uncles and at least one of my cousins have either experienced, or been diagnosed with manic depression. I don't know how far back this goes as I've never checked my ancestry. But the illness is so prevalent in my immediate family that it has to be genetic.

For me, this was like a sword of Damocles. The family black cloud hanging over me, if you like. I found this knowledge extremely difficult to comprehend when I was growing up and struggled to come to terms with it. To me it was a kind of death sentence, an omen of what was to come.

Faye: Was your father's side also affected?

My father's relatives are harder to trace. He left home at about fourteen and lost contact with his family. But I understand, that his grandmother had problems. She was either schizophrenic, or had some other severe mental illness that affected her life. Whether this was clinically diagnosed or not, I don't know. But I do remember him talking about her and saying that she was often quite disturbed. As this was never researched, I don't know for sure. But he did have quite a difficult childhood himself that was never really talked about.

Alastair: Talking of genetics, I have a secondary illness – diabetes. As far as I know, there is no genetic basis for this, no hereditary link whatsoever. But as in any illness, I have to take precautions against a setback. I'm not the world's best at staying vigilant though. Let's face it, I have a few bad habits that I'd actually like to hang on to!

But the business of genetics and the family connection to manic depression is fascinating. Perhaps worthy of even more research in the future.

Chris's View

A typical question that arises from working with service users, their families, or with anyone discussing mental illness is, 'What is the cause?' The examination of possible causes can lead to a whole series of problems in themselves, often triggering guilt, blame and recrimination between family members. All types of theories are applied in the search for the answer, which is very often a waste of time and can be very destructive.

Adam said, *'I believe that no single event caused the illness that crippled me later'.* A great deal of time, energy and self-examination (when people reflect upon their childhood and early development) is contained within this brief statement. To attribute all the complications of bipolar disorder to one event in childhood lacks evidence. Questions around bullying, divorce, birth order etc. quickly appear insignificant when you meet a service user ten or twenty years later experiencing a manic episode.

The general ambiguity around the issue and the problem of identifying factors that may, or may not, have played a part in the illness developing leads to an unnecessary focus. The focus should be about the person's recovery and managing the disorder itself.

Parents and close relatives often experience a strong sense of guilt and spend long periods of time wondering what they could have done to prevent the onset. These periods of self-examination can be extremely difficult and are often characterised by family conflict, self-blame and fear. For those diagnosed, the most common question has to be, *'Was there something in my childhood that might have caused this illness?'*

The short answer is no, there most likely isn't.

For many people this view is far too simplistic; however, this is due to a subjective view about what mental illness actually is, and is not linked to the evidence about possible causes.

Alongside major stressors such as losing a job, divorce or bereavement, there are the effects of biological changes; poor sleep, poor diet, even the stress of living in an argumentative household. All these have an impact on mood. Trying to identify a single cause is a pointless exercise. It is the interplay between these factors and the individual which can trigger episodes of mania or depression.

As you read the accounts of Adam, Faye and Alastair's childhoods, you may conclude little about the illness itself in terms of a single definitive cause. You may also conclude that their backgrounds are so different that they share little or nothing in common. However, there are certain key features and significant events within their accounts that, combined with a strong genetic vulnerability, make further examination essential.

Research has established that bipolar disorder has no single proven cause. The illness appears to be due to changes in the way some nerve cells function in the brain, affecting communication and cognitive awareness. Whatever the precise biochemical nature, the disorder makes people far more vulnerable to emotional and physical stress, and significantly impairs their thinking.

By themselves, isolated incidents from childhood do not provide us with a clear understanding of what might have caused Adam, Faye and Alastair's later mental health problems. From the genetic viewpoint, far more reliable indicators as to possible causes can be found in their family histories:

» Faye's father was diagnosed with depression
» Adam had two uncles and a cousin diagnosed with bipolar disorder
» Alastair's grandmother may have committed suicide.
» Adam's grandmother (on his father's side) had apparent mental health issues

Bipolar disorder in children and adolescents (particularly prepubescent children) often presents a sizeable challenge to health professionals. Diagnosis should be made by a clinician with specialist training in child and adolescent mental health, after consultation with all relevant parties. The more information that can be assessed using the guidelines mentioned above, the better prepared the clinician will be in making an accurate diagnosis and, from there, to recommend appropriate treatment.

Adolescence

"If I'd known what I was going to go through
later I'm not sure I'd have wanted to carry on'

1. How did your teenage years affect your illness?

Faye: From the age of about thirteen I was withdrawn, and just threw myself into my schoolwork. I literally used to come home from school, do my homework, then go out and walk the streets for an hour or two, just to get away from the house. I got on well with my teachers, because I was obviously putting a lot of effort into my work. But there were one or two who were quite concerned, mainly because I would sit and not interact with any of the other children. My schoolwork was perfect. It was the social side that was completely lacking.

Adam: You didn't make friends easily, then?

Not really. I just remember wanting to be on my own most of the time. From thirteen to eighteen this was pretty much a regular feature of my life. But then, I thought everyone felt like that. My mum would tell me to pull myself together and get on with it, and I would think, what am I doing wrong? How come everyone else can cope with it? It was an awful time, really, looking back. A time I'd much rather forget.

Alastair: My teenage years were spent at boarding school. I didn't see my parents for long periods but I had, to some extent, got used to this by then. The bed-wetting still occurred for a couple of years, though. Even at thirteen I hadn't grown out of that. It wouldn't be so frequent, but it would still be there.

But I don't recall any dramatic changes in my mood during that time. As I said before, all I cared about was having a good time. Lessons didn't interest me at all. When I was in the classroom, all I would think about was, Oh, God – when is this lesson going to end? When is this boring old fart going to stop droning on about physics, or the universe, or whatever! I couldn't concentrate. I had no interest in learning whatsoever. I just liked to bait the teachers. You know, make them look a bit stupid and all that. Make it difficult for them in some way. Incorrigible might be the best description of my behaviour back then.

Faye: You were a bit of a bad boy, then?

No, not really. I just loved being the class clown. I don't think I was any different from any other child at that age, just a lot lazier. And I was popular, too. I wasn't seen as a threat in any way. I was okay at sports – cricket and rugby. I had no real problems joining-in in that respect.

But my academic record was horrendous. You can chart my decline at school by looking at my grades over the next few terms. When I first went to Epsom I went into the B grade. But every year I dropped a grade, from B to C, and the following year to D. The teachers were appalled by my complete lack of interest.

I wasn't a complete failure though. At the time there was this logic test that was done throughout the Oxbridge public schools. We all had to do it. So I took this test and didn't think much more about it. Then, I can remember being called in by the Headmaster and told that I'd actually got a hundred percent. Only two people throughout the entire public schools system had achieved this distinction and I was one of them!

Adam: That's quite remarkable, given your lack of motivation.

Well, yes, absolutely! And of course, the Headmaster wanted to know why. Here was this perennial joker, who'd been failing so badly in the classroom, who was clearly quite intelligent. Again, it was just that I liked playing the fool. The exam results indicated that I had a brain, I just wasn't prepared to use it!

By then I'd gone beyond caring. Plus, I had another huge distraction to take my mind off lessons. Girls came into the school. Not that many, but enough to make an impact on the lower sixth.

Faye: And you did your best to entertain them?

Naturally! I was reasonably successful, too, but that's another story. But the pranks and the larking about were getting out of hand. I couldn't go anywhere without some accusation of misconduct being thrown at me. The truth is, I revelled in this notoriety, but it did have its downside, that's for sure.

Adam: Around this time, something happened that is pivotal for me. While I was at Secondary school, around the age of thirteen or fourteen, I had an episode of what I would now call clinical depression. I can remember going to school and having to sit in a classroom in this terrible state, unable to speak, unable to smile. You've seen pictures of depressives, where the face is immobile and the eyes are hooded, well, that was me. I had no energy, no capacity to fight what was happening. It was dreadful. A truly frightening experience to go through.

This particular episode lasted for about a week, then left of its own accord. There were no pills, no medical intervention. I didn't discuss it with anyone, but struggled through it as best I could. But it made a huge impact on me. It affected everything. I would lie awake at night, unable to sleep, plagued by this terrible sickness that wouldn't leave me. The whole thing was characterised by fear. This all consuming fear. I found the prospect of a reoccurrence terrifying.

Faye: Did anything trigger this episode?

Not that I can remember. I had problems at school like everyone else, but nothing terrible. It was just something that came along out of the blue and radically affected my whole life. If I'd known what I was going to go through later I'm not sure I'd have wanted to carry on.

2. Did you find interacting with other people difficult or easy?

Alastair: In general, I found it quite easy. My more outrageous behaviour certainly endeared me to a large section of the population at school, and I enjoyed that. I thrived in an atmosphere of games and joking around. But equally, I wasn't afraid to be on my own or anything like that. I wasn't running away from anything as far as I could tell.

Adam: You see your teenage years as reasonably well balanced, then?

Yes, on the whole. When I compare my adolescence to later periods in my life when I was definitely out of control, then yes, I was quite well balanced. I seemed to have had no major issues to contend with. No black depression as you described. No major psychological problems.

Faye: I so wish I'd had your confidence when I was at school. As I said, my house was a war zone. Dad was depressed, and he'd go around slamming doors and shouting. He was completely off-the-wall. He couldn't relate to any of us in a normal way. Mum was trying to hold it all together and look after my little brother. Consequently, I would spend a great deal of time out of the house. I'd even sit on a park bench for hours on end, thinking.

Alastair: You felt quite alienated at the time, then?

Very much so, yes. The few friends I had at the time said they couldn't cope. In fact, from the age of about fourteen onwards, I don't think I had any friends at all. They'd all given up on me by that point. School seemed to magnify all the personal problems I had and made them harder to cope with. I felt the sense of isolation really strongly.

Adam: I had a mixed attitude to school. I enjoyed Art and Creative Writing and excelled at these without too much effort. I found most other lessons boring and, like Alastair, tended to be disruptive in the classroom. But I did make several close friends. And there were always girls to take your mind off the lessons. I remember falling in love with a girl in my class who spurned my advances and went out with someone else. I used to walk past her house on the way home from school feeling destitute. I'm not sure how a broken heart compares to clinical depression but the pain is certainly memorable.

My home life was fairly stable. I had good relations with my family, although things were strained with my dad at times. He was the disciplinarian, quick tempered and quick to lash out if you wound him up at the wrong time. In many ways I was a typical teenager. I listened to the Top Forty religiously every Sunday night and lined my bedroom wall with Bruce Lee posters from *Kung Fu Monthly*. School was stressful at times, but, looking back, I suppose it was bearable. I wasn't bullied or anything.

Alastair: Bullying was rife at public school. It was an accepted thing in the hierarchy, a sort of rites of passage everyone went through. Thankfully, I wasn't bullied like some of the other children. But there was one incident that happened to me that was really quite appalling.

One evening, I was dragged from the dormitory by two other boys and pushed into a bath of scalding water. I was burned quite severely as a result and needed medical attention. But that was pretty much an isolated incident and didn't reflect the overall nature of my schooling.

Faye: God, that's awful. That must have had a profound affect upon you, surely?

Obviously it was a terrible shock to me at the time. But I don't believe it had any lasting effect. It didn't make me more introverted or frightened of other boys. I just accepted it had happened and moved on.

Adam: Thankfully, nothing like that happened to me. Apart from the odd smack in the mouth from jealous boyfriends, the bullies generally left me alone.

I did have a few close friendships with boys in my year. And obviously girls were a huge distraction, as I said. But I had no outward problems that I can remember.

The depressive episodes I suffered didn't seem to affect that aspect of my life in any way. I seemed to recover fairly quickly and moved on. But I always felt that cloud hanging over me. This is one of the problems you face when you come

'I just loved being the class clown. I don't think I was any different from any other child at that age, just a lot lazier.'

out of a depressive phase. If your mood lowers slightly, you think, oh God, it must be happening again.

Faye: How about hobbies and interests? Where there any major influences during this period?'

Yes, the outbreak of Punk music in the '70s. This had a huge impact on me at school, around the age of fourteen, fifteen. There was this small underground movement, consisting of a few fellow subversives, all swapping singles and bootleg tapes in the classroom. A friend of mine brought me in a copy of the Sex Pistols *Never Mind the Bollocks* album, in a plain white sleeve. I took it home one lunchtime, thinking my dad was out, and put it on the turntable. He walked in and went ballistic! The Sex Pistols, and all those Punk bands, were an affront to his generation and he couldn't deal with it. But to me that just made the whole thing more attractive.

The era had a profound effect on me. I loved the whole anarchic spirit of the movement, The Stranglers in particular who were unique in their look and sound. How this violent and aggressive music affected my fragile mental state I have no idea, but I certainly threw myself into it wholeheartedly at the time.

Alastair: Punk had a huge effect on me, as well. In fact, the first album I ever bought was *Rattus Norvegicus* by The Stranglers. I even started dressing up, wearing safety pins and jackets with padlocks. King's Cross in '77 was an amazing place to be. A few of us would head up there during holidays and check out Malcolm McLaren's shop, staring at all the fascinating characters you'd see going in and out. The music and the rebellion certainly summed up the spirit of my generation, without a doubt.

3. How did you relate to other members of your family?

Faye: We were a very small unit. My grandma was alive at the time, but she was living up in Yorkshire and I only saw her about once a year. My other grandparents had died. I did have quite a lot of contact with my aunt and uncle, who lived in Swindon. I'd often go and stay with them for a week, just to get away from the house for a bit. Whenever Mum needed a break, she'd send me off to Aunt Janet and Uncle Vic.

Adam: Did you find it a relief to be away from the house at that point?

Yes, very much so. I mean, their place was a madhouse, really. They had three small kids, my cousins, running around, so it was chaotic. But, I always felt a bit of release when I went there, glad of the change in environment. Of course, they made a fuss of me as well, which made me feel I was special again. I suppose it was like having another family in a way, although I didn't see it like that at the time. Sadly, I'm not in touch with them anymore, though. You drift apart, and life takes you in different directions. But I do look back on those days with fondness. Perhaps I felt truly happy there in some way, I don't really know.

Alastair: My two older sisters were also at boarding at the same time as me. I would see them when we had *exeats* – which were like weekend breaks you had every six weeks or so. Once I went to see my sister, who was living in London. She was actually living with three gay men. This was the first time I had ever met homosexuals, as such, so it was a bit of a culture shock, to say the least. But they seemed really nice and, as I said before, I found it easy to get on with people no matter who they were.

Life for me at the time was pretty good. My sisters mothered me a little bit, because my parents were still abroad, and I would see them in London whenever I could.

Generally speaking, I had no real problems at all.

Then, when I was eighteen, the first real traumatic episode of my life happened. I got expelled from Epsom. This was a devastating blow for me really. I knew that I'd disappointed my parents. I knew that they had to pay quite a lot of money for me to go to school. But that was it. The decision was final. I wasn't even allowed to take my A levels there.

The Headmaster called me in and said, in this pompous, melodramatic voice, 'Donald, if you had made it to five years at Epsom College, you would have made a joke of the entire public school system!'

And with that, I believe I got a beating.

Adam: So beatings were prevalent at public school?

Oh yes, very much so. I've even had the split cane, which I believe was abolished hundreds of years ago. I actually got that as a punishment for some minor transgression. I remember being beaten by the Headmaster who I'd infuriated. Although I got six strokes, I had twelve blood marks as a result. So he'd used the split cane on me, without a doubt.

Faye: That sounds absolutely barbaric!

It was. But back then, certain 'traditions', for want of a better word, were acceptable. You just went along with it, thinking it was normal.

Adam: I can sympathise to a degree. I had the cane a few times at secondary school. The Head of Year, who shall remain nameless, used to make a ritual of it. He'd call you into his study and tell you to put your hands on his desk and spread your feet apart. You'd know exactly what you had coming – and it hurt, too! You wouldn't forget that in a hurry.

Faye: Thankfully, I didn't experience anything like that at the schools I went to. But, I do look back on that period of my life as being extremely unsettled and unhappy. And, I'd yet to experience some of the more destructive influences that crippled me later on. The bulimia, and the mood swings that led to my later diagnosis of bipolar.

Chris's View

As previously stated, identifying bipolar disorder in children and adolescents – particularly prepubescent children – presents a considerable challenge.

The current diagnostic process, developed for adults, has limitations when applied to the younger age group. For this reason, the guidance of a clinician experienced in this area should be sought before any decision is made regarding treatment. I have known cases where a diagnosis of bipolar disorder referred more to personality traits rather than actual shifts in mood.

The peak age of onset of bipolar disorder tends to be in late adolescence or early adulthood, with a small increase in incidence in mid-to late life. We could conclude, perhaps, that incidents of bullying, feeling isolated, and being separated from family members are obvious trigger factors, but this is not borne out by the evidence.

A great deal of research has taken place examining the impact of psychological trauma and the development of psychosis, as well as a range of other disorders. Trauma can disrupt an individual's life by creating a block in cognitive and emotional processing, this includes regulation of feelings.

The significance of stress in the stress vulnerability model is also a crucial component. Stress can be viewed as a subjective experience and can have physiological and psychological effects on a person. It can be viewed as a force that impacts on the individual, placing them under strain with undesirable consequences. Stress can fall into three categories:

» Stimulus
» Response
» Interaction between an individual and their environment

Within the stress-vulnerability model, stress is deemed changeable, a factor which influences the manifestation of symptoms. This is broken down into Ambient and Life Event Stress. Ambient Stress can impact an individual throughout their daily lives, whether great or small. Life Event Stress refers to specific events that cause high levels of stress.

Adam's reported episode of low mood aged fourteen is significant when we look at his overall life experience.

» Vividly describes a week-long period during which he didn't speak (mute)
» Didn't smile (loss of facial expression)
» Was fearful (anxiety)

From the clear diagnostic guidelines we have, it seems obvious that he was suffering from depression.

Does this follow on, then, that he would develop bipolar disorder as a consequence?

The NICE Guidelines (2006) indicate that both Adam and Faye, in particular, could warrant further attention due to the risk factors apparent in their family backgrounds. *'Adolescents with a history of depression and a family history of bipolar disorder should be carefully followed up.'* (NICE 2006)

Under these guidelines, an assessment of Adam, aged 14, would have included:

» A detailed mental state examination, based on an

interview

» A medical evaluation to exclude organic causes

» Further neuropsychological and neurological evaluation, as appropriate

» A detailed account of the presenting problem from the child, parents or carers, and other significant adults, such as teachers

» A detailed developmental and neurodevelopmental history, including birth history, speech and language development, behaviour problems, attachment behaviour and any history of abuse. (NICE 2006)

Although the illness has a clear genetic component, Bauer (2003) concludes that 'Genetics is not destiny'. This tells us that, despite the research, the predictability of the disorder remains elusive. Such inconclusive findings does little to reassure family members bewildered by the onset of the illness and leaves many unanswered questions. Some of these will be discussed throughout this book.

The Hereditary Factor

'These dark forces within me seemed to take
over, leaving me with the feeling I had no
control over my own destiny'

1. Do you have a history of mental illness in your family?

Alastair: I suppose I'm quite unique in a way. I've had to come to terms with the fact that I'm the only certified lunatic the Donald's have ever had! But seriously, I'd have to say no, there's never been mental illness in my family. Not to my knowledge, anyway.

I did used to wonder where the strong religious obsession came from. The sort of delusions that are common to mania, and to some extent depression. My own experiences with this kind of thinking came about much later, during my manic phases. Then I would feel a god-like transcendence and would feel compelled to act out in all sorts of ways. But, I certainly had no insight into my behaviour at the time. And no one in my family history to compare that behaviour to, either.

Adam: Strange how religious mania is a recognised feature of bipolar disorder.

Yes, it is. I wasn't brought up in any kind of faith, although religion was forced on us at school, though. We had to attend church every Sunday and listen to boring old sermons. But most of the boys treated it as a bit of a joke. I remember sliding along on the shiny pews and being told to sit still. But it didn't stop me for long.

I think I was quite distrustful of religious people back then and tended not to have anything to do with them. I saw it all as one more attempt to control me, which, up until then, the teachers had been unable to do.

Faye: I can't say that I had any particular obsession with religion. Mine was a sort of inner turmoil, based around the problems I had at the time. It took me years to come to terms with the fact that my brain doesn't work properly. I always thought that it was something I'd done, or something I was reacting to. I didn't appreciate that my brain chemistry is different than other people. That it's not my fault. You know – I've picked this up from my dad and there's nothing I can do about it. It took me a long time to come to terms with that.

Alastair: So there was a history in your family, then?

Well, yes. My dad suffered badly with depression for years, as I said before. I'm not sure if this was hereditary, but it certainly had an impact on the rest of the family.

Also, I struggled with bulimia for sixteen years. I know this is from a mainly female perspective and not something directly related to manic depression, but it did consume a large part of my life. A lot of women comfort eat when depressed. Plus, there are a lot of medications out there that cause weight gain and increased appetite. From about the age of 20 to 36, I fluctuated between the extremes, binging and putting on weight while depressed, dieting and exercising to excess when manic.

Alastair: Do you see this as part of your manic depression or separate?

Mainly separate, although there probably is a link if you go right back to its primary causes. But other women I've met have had weight issues too, Anorexia also being common. Eating disorders can be seen as another form of self-harm and trying to control mood. That was certainly how I used it.

Adam: I find it fascinating, how we all come from completely different backgrounds and yet we share this illness. My family history had a profound effect on how I saw things. I viewed all forms of mental illness as a curse or punishment and wondered what I'd done to deserve it. There was a strong religious component too. I was brought up in what you might call a divided household – certainly where matters of faith were concerned. My father was either atheist or agnostic, I'm not sure which. My mother, on the other hand, was a practising Christian. This caused quite a few arguments between them and left a strained atmosphere that I picked up on as a child.

Later, I began to associate my black depressions as a sign that I was inherently bad, that I must have done something pretty awful to be singled out for such a punishment. This religious theme stayed with me on and off for many years, fuelling an obsession with death and the afterlife. Most of the time I was sitting round waiting for the black cloud to come back again.

Faye: Almost as a divine retribution?

In many ways yes. As I said, this underlying religious theme was there from childhood on. Not that I took any comfort from it. My mother's Christian faith influenced family life to quite an extent. Certain books or TV programmes would be frowned upon, as would any foul language or explicit reference to sex. I accepted this as being perfectly normal until I started mixing with other kids and going to their houses. Here, I found a much more diverse range of moral values and in some cases, far less censorship in the home.

I remember being about twelve or thirteen at a friend's house one lunchtime and listening to a *Derek and Clive* record. What shocked me more than the language was the fact that my friend's dad owned the record! Here we were – two school kids – giggling away in his front room, listening to all this foul-mouthed abuse, and to him it was perfectly acceptable. Incidents like this made me question my own upbringing and in particular the religious beliefs that were such an influential part of it.

Alastair: I think that's an interesting point, regarding the genetic question. How much we are influenced by our upbringing and environment. I didn't have religious beliefs forced on me by my parents, but I was always aware of things like morality and censorship from a young age. I think it's important that children make their own minds up about issues like religion and don't have their thinking done for them. But whether a person's upbringing could trigger something as devastating as manic depression, I don't know.

Adam: This question has intrigued me for many years, especially in the light of my own experience. Could my illness have been caused, in part, by my upbringing? Was religion a contributory factor? My continuing obsession with death and the afterlife certainly made me a prime candidate for depression that's for sure.

But I have to say that the hereditary theory is pretty convincing. We know that we inherit certain physical characteristics from our parents, so why not the capacity for mental illness also? I had a fascination with themes that might be considered unhealthy in a child today, but I don't think that this on its own caused me to be manic depressive. These dark forces within me seemed to take over, leaving me with the feeling I had no control over my own destiny.

Faye: The same theme of retribution again?

Yes, definitely. The deeper I went into my own depression, the more I came to see it as a curse, without a doubt. I could see no benefits to it at all, only how damaging it was to me as a person. To be struck down by something so powerful and debilitating in adolescence made me see the world in dark colours. I really did live in a sort of twilight zone half the time, wondering when my next bout was going to come. The family connection made it even more final. I couldn't see a way out.

2. Does the hereditary link make the illness harder to treat?

Faye: No matter what I've been through in terms of mental illness or eating disorders, I've never stopped trying. I've had some good doctors over the years as well, who've been really understanding. In fact I'm working with a really good counsellor at the moment, and I'm learning so much about the condition – what I can do and how I can change things. So I'm optimistic about the future. I know my own strengths as well as my weaknesses. I'm never going to be the sort to have a wide circle of friends and what have you, but that's okay. I'm happy with the way I am. Or at least, I've reached a kind of acceptance.

Adam: Your limitations don't stop you making progress?

That's right. I mean I still keep trying, no matter what. Next year, I'm hoping to go to university, so that will mean social

'I certainly had no insight into my behaviour at the time. And no one in my family history to compare that behaviour to either.'

interaction again, and mixing with strangers. But, I'm hoping that, by then, I'll be so much further along in getting better. I'll be able to cope with the changes. The fact, is that now I can plan this kind of thing. Not so long ago, I wouldn't have been able to. I didn't have the stability.

Alastair: Not having any previous history in my own family, my own case is harder to analyse. Or perhaps it's easier, depending which way you look at it. Without any genetic link, my early symptoms must have developed from an outside cause, similar to those we discussed earlier. My environment or my social habits. Drug taking, for instance. I know that smoking cannabis causes psychosis in some people and distorts the thinking to a degree.

But in terms of successful treatment, I wouldn't think the hereditary link makes any difference. Once you've been diagnosed manic depressive, that's it. It doesn't matter how you got it. You either respond to a course of treatment or you don't.

Adam: I've often wondered how the hereditary aspect affects my own illness. Whether this makes it more resistant to treatment, I don't know. I understand that there are varying severities in manic depression and that not everyone responds to treatment the same way. I prefer to think that positive lifestyle changes, either with or without medication, are the best defence against another episode. But it's taken me a number of very bleak and self-destructive years to reach that conclusion.

Faye: Did you resort to self-medicating early in your illness?

Not at first. At least not intentionally. From the age of about fourteen on, my drug of choice was always alcohol. I used it to mask a lot of painful feelings and to fit in socially. I can remember feeling really awkward in social situations, not knowing how to act or what to say. Alcohol gave me the courage to get over that. But of course there's a price to pay in the long run. I didn't think there was anything wrong with my coping strategies at the time. Everyone I knew seemed to drink like I did. The true extent of the problem wasn't revealed until later on.

Alastair: I think the temptation to self-medicate must be common for manic depressives, especially in the early stages. Particularly if you haven't been diagnosed and have no history in your family. I suppose it's different for me, in that my illness was quite possibly caused by recreational drug use at some stage. Unfortunately, there's no way of knowing which drug is going to affect which person. Everyone reacts in different ways. Perhaps certain people are more susceptible to mental illness than others.

What I will say, is that during episodes of mania, your ability to think clearly is drastically reduced. I can remember being in America and thinking I was the Chosen One. I'd walk down the street expecting people to bow down before me. The feeling was incredible. Much more powerful than any drug I could have taken. In depression, your perceptions are also distorted but in the opposite way. Depression is the other end of the spectrum. It's painful and you'd do anything to relieve that pain.

3. If there is a hereditary link, how do you feel about the possibility of passing the illness on to your children?

Faye: Well, as I don't have children it isn't something I have to worry about. But it did put me off having any initially, I must admit. I couldn't bear the thought of them inheriting the gene – if there is one.

Although I do tend to think, well, I'm doing okay at the moment so maybe it's not that bad, I know this isn't a true reflection of the severity of the illness. Yes, you can learn to live with it as an individual, but would you want to inflict the same upheaval on a child?

A lot of progress has been made over the last ten years, with research and new treatments, so there are reasons to be optimistic about the future. But I always feel it's a delicate balancing act.

I did this awareness course a while ago, and met all these other bipolars. The vast majority of us were creative, dynamic people. Writing, music, art. The whole spectrum. It really was amazing to find so many of us linked in this way. You have to appreciate that this is the other side of it, that it's not all bad. I mean there are times when I absolutely love being bipolar. There is no feeling like it. But the thought of your own children going through the same thing is almost unbearable. Something you don't want to consider.

Adam: What about genetics and the promise of research?

Regarding gene testing, and whatever they might come up with in the future, I don't know. I'm a scientist. Having spent years working in laboratories I'm all up for research as the way forward. But it's like Frankenstein's monster, isn't it. How much do we play around with our own biology in the name of improvement? How far do we go?

Alastair: I don't think we should mess with nature, to be honest. But that's just my own personal view. There are times I've seen manic depression as a huge curse. Then, like Faye, there are also times I've seen it as a great blessing. If you said to me, would you rather avoid being bipolar? I don't know how I would answer. There have been times of such elation that I've experienced through the manic phase, which have been so phenomenal, so extraordinary and so powerful, that I'm glad I had them. They really were that memorable. Stronger than any drug I've ever taken. And I've taken quite a few drugs in my time, I'm quite happy to admit that.

Faye: You feel the experience has enhanced your life that much?

Well, I certainly regret the disruption the illness has caused my family. But the experience itself has given me a deeper awareness, an understanding of the extremes I can go to in my own mind. The idea of genetics, in terms of treatment, raises a lot of questions for me. I'm not sure I agree with scientists or doctors, tampering with human nature. To produce what – a clone? Someone born with a fundamental part of their character missing?

But in saying that, I wouldn't miss the depressive side of the illness. The weeks and months of lying around without the energy to do anything. That really is awful. Depression is the price you pay for the heights you go to during mania. At that time you're so alive you're untouchable. It's the other end of the spectrum. The complete opposite in terms of energy and creativity.

Adam: I suppose it's almost the same question with medication. How much would you want to suppress your children's feelings, impulses and thought processes? Medication provides a lifeline for people with severe illnesses. But, as you say, sometimes there's a price to pay in terms of personal freedom. Playing God is a risky business. I don't know how far genetic research is able to go in finding a solution, but there has to be an ethical dilemma here. Denying a child the experience of manic depression by tampering with genetics may well be morally wrong, but the devastation caused by the illness also needs to be looked at. There has to be some sort of balance. And, like you, Alastair, I wouldn't want my children to go through the same experiences.

The experts say there's been a significant increase in the illness over the last fifty or so years. If this is the case, what's the cause? Is the increase due to societal factors, such as the population explosion or the demise of the nuclear family? I think it's interesting to look at the problem in a social context. There are so many different factors involved in every case study. Science doesn't hold all the answers.

Faye: Are you against genetic testing overall?

That's a difficult question. I think with other diseases, particularly those with a hereditary link, it's easier to be an advocate. Everyone would like to see diseases like Parkinson's and Huntington's eradicated, that goes without saying. I have direct experience of Huntington's in my own family and I know the devastation it causes. But manic depression is such a complex illness in terms of its effect on the individual. Then there's the cultural aspect. How many great works of Art have been created during the heights of mania? How many writers and artists owe their success, in part, to the profound nature of their illness? Not to mention ordinary members of society whose careers have been enhanced in the same way. In terms of any genetic breakthrough, I think we need to ask how much we stand to lose rather than how much we might gain.

Chris's View

Like other complex inherited conditions, bipolar disorder only occurs in a fraction of the individuals at genetic risk. This, in itself, questions the belief that the disorder is solely genetic in origin. Attempting to attribute the illness to one single factor is to miss its inherent complexity. Although there appears to be a strong genetic link, this factor becomes unreliable when we look at those who eventually go on to develop symptoms in later life.

Below are some general facts about the illness.

» Affects around 1-1.5% of the population (Bebbington, 1995)
» Costs NHS £200m in treatment and societal costs of £2billion a year (Gupra et al, 2002)
» Mean age of onset is early to mid 20s
» Similar prevalence for men and women
» Characterised, for many, by repeated episodes (rates of 80%-90% of repeated episodes)

Adam, Faye and Alastair all experienced some disturbance in childhood (Alastair's separation from his parents at an early age, Faye's being bullied at school). And yet, if attending public school or being bullied were factors in causation, this would be reflected in significant increases in the general population. There is also the matter of perception.

Faye reports feeling isolated from her peers during childhood, but claims to have enjoyed her schoolwork. She discusses her experience of being bullied and reflects that her childhood was not happy for her at all. However, many children experience similar distress without going on to develop mental illness. Alastair's traumatic scalding incident at public school might well have been a causative factor in later psychological problems, and yet he minimises the incident, claiming that it was an unfortunate aspect of the broader culture prevalent at the time.

Bipolar disorder is a serious mental health illness which is recognised by the International Classification of Diseases 10 (World Health Organisation 2010). An individual who suffers from bipolar disorder will experience severe mood swings during which they will experience either a manic or depressive phase that may last for several weeks or months (Royal College of Psychiatrists 2012). It is not fully understood what causes bipolar, but research suggests that there is a physical difference in the brain which controls mood.

Several studies have used neuroimaging techniques to highlight structural or functional changes in the brain where the individual has a diagnosis of bipolar.

The Royal College of Psychiatrists (2012) say that bipolar disorder may be genetic, or may be caused by personal stressful experiences. The combination of life events and genetic factors can trigger the illness. A great deal of your time can be spent on identifying single causes; however, it is far more effective to manage the experiences and prevent relapse. In their discussions, you can see how Faye, Alastair and Adam do this.

Sex

'Yes, I have much more confidence, that goes without saying. That is one aspect of the illness that can get me into a lot of trouble'

1. How has bipolar disorder influenced your sexual behaviour?

Alastair: That's a difficult question. I don't think it really has. I know that might be the total opposite of other manic depressives' experiences, but that's how it is for me.

When I'm busy – high, or manic, whatever you want to call it – sex doesn't really interest me. I just see it as a physical thing that you can do, whereas the feelings in my head are a lot more exciting to me than sex is. This isn't a reflection of my sex drive in general, obviously. But certainly during the height of mania.

Adam: You're describing a facet of the manic phase, where you almost go beyond physical pleasure?

Absolutely. That's exactly how I feel. In fact you couldn't have put it better.

Faye: I had a brief period when I was nineteen, or twenty, when I became much more outgoing. I wasn't promiscuous, but I was more open to having relationships. Before, I just didn't have the confidence. Around that time I became more willing to go out and find someone. But I always got to know them first; I was never into one-night stands or anything. Looking back, I was definitely more relaxed about sex and relationships around this time.

Alastair: Because your mood had changed?

Yes. I was starting to come up for the first time, after many years suffering depression. But, as I said, I didn't become promiscuous or reckless because of it. You hear all these stories of bipolars running off with their next door neighbours, or sleeping with total strangers, and that must be awful. Thankfully, that didn't happen to me.

For me, sex is something you do with someone you love, and I was able to hang onto that no matter what else was going on at the time.

A lot of it is down to your upbringing, isn't it? I was brought up by my dad, who was quite strict. You don't swear, you don't sleep around, you work hard. That was the philosophy he passed on to me. The illness does distort your thinking, especially during mania, but most of the time I was able to keep that side of things under control.

Adam: The manic phase can be devastating in terms of personal relationships. Your inhibitions go. You become more sociable. You're more inclined to talk to people – complete strangers even. For me, it became delusional. I would become so super-confident in my ability to attract the opposite sex that the thought of failure never entered my mind. As far as I was concerned, women were put there solely for my personal pleasure whenever I felt the urge. A pretty distorted view of reality I know, but it's an incredible feeling. You almost become a super being. You're no longer a part of the human race, but something far beyond it.

Alastair: Adam – I could not have put it better myself. A Super Being. That's exactly what you become!

Yes, but it does have its downside. I met this woman once and arranged to meet her in a pub later that evening. Being manic at the time and not thinking rationally, I turned up late and barged in on her as she was talking to a group of friends. Instead of apologising and trying to be sociable, I asked if I could borrow some money to buy a drink. She wasn't very happy about it, to say the least.

Depression has the opposite effect, of course. As Alastair said, you just want to hide away. You've got no interest in anything. Sometimes sex can be a distraction from the pain of what you're going through, but it can only be temporary.

2. How dangerous is the loss of inhibition during mania?

Faye: I think I've been lucky in some respects. Most of the times I've been high, I've been in a serious relationship, firstly with my husband, and with my current partner. He's been my rock. He understands how the illness comes and goes, and the different aspects of it that affect my character. He actually loves it when I'm uninhibited, so long as I'm not out of control. But as I said before, I haven't had any really humiliating experiences like Adam's, thankfully.

Alastair: You had some insight into your moods, then, even when you were manic?

To some extent, yes, although the medical profession might dispute that!

I had my first manic episode around the age of eighteen, or nineteen. Since then I've found an outlet in other things – like running, for instance – that help channel my excess energy. Sex, for me, was never that big a thing. It was something I always felt I was saving, for the time I was in a safe situation.

I do agree that being manic changes your attitude to the physical side of sex. It's just one more outlet, a distraction you can do without. All that effort involved in pursuing a relationship. You're too busy. You're happy in your own mind and you don't particularly need anything or anyone else.

In terms of mental stimulation, mania is all-consuming, about as powerful as it gets. The danger for me would be in meeting the wrong person during these times, and making the wrong decision while my thinking wasn't straight.

Alastair: In terms of how I relate to women, it's different. Yes, I have much more confidence, that goes without saying. I don't really see it as a sexual thing, though. It's more a part of my busy nature, one more aspect of my mania. But I do get much more aggressive, more outspoken. So, yes, that is one aspect of the illness that can get me into a lot of trouble.

Faye: Do you go out of your way to seduce women when you're like this?

What – all that running around wasting all my precious energy? I'm far too lazy for all that!
But no, seriously, if I see someone who looks interesting, regardless of whether I find them sexually attractive or not, I'm quite happy to go and talk to them. And I feel very confident in that. Confident in every single thing I do – when I'm busy. When I'm not busy, it's the opposite. I can be a scared little rabbit who wants to hide away from everyone.

So for me, the loss of inhibition in mania isn't necessarily linked to sexual promiscuity, but to a general lack of awareness, a willingness to put myself in potentially dangerous situations without even thinking about it.

'For me, it became delusional. I would become so super-confident in my ability to attract the opposite sex that the thought of failure never entered my mind'

Adam: It does seem to be common, certainly from our accounts, that the manic phase almost suppresses the sexual urge. Basically, your mood is so elevated you haven't the time to stop and engage in any kind of intense physical activity. It's difficult to describe that state to someone who hasn't experienced it. The chaotic overload of your thinking. The way your thoughts are moving so fast, it's a job to catch up with them.

But it's your intentions, your reckless behaviour that makes it so dangerous. That's why marriages break up. Your partner can't stand the strain of being around someone so self-destructive.

Going back to what Alastair said about being aggressive during mania. I remember pursuing women when I was manic, without any regard whatsoever to the consequences. God knows how I haven't been murdered by outraged husbands or boyfriends, because I just didn't care. The fact that I was married didn't matter either. I was up and running, doing whatever I wanted whenever I felt like it. The feeling of superiority is incredible.

But the physical side – the actual seduction and jumping into bed routine – involved too much effort. I was usually far too busy to stop for all that.

Faye: That's certainly been my experience. During the height of mania, you don't need any extra stimulation.

Alastair: Exactly. It's almost as if the super being doesn't really care about it. The mind has gone beyond sex. In this state, your thoughts are free flowing. It's like having a mental orgasm, for want of a better description. You're on such a colossal high.

But it's always your partner who suffers most. Especially when you're on a mission, so to speak. Perhaps you've been up for days without sleep, and staying out all hours with all kinds of strange people. I've been lucky to have a really supportive partner, who's stuck by me throughout, in spite of my frequent flights into full-blown mania and the chaos that brings.

Adam: Yes, it is always those closest to you who bear the brunt. My wife put up with years of upheaval because of my illness and the consequences of that. The loss of inhibition common in mania is one of the hardest things for a partner to understand. The increased confidence and distorted sense of well-being you feel leads you to some strange places in your head. Things you wouldn't conceive of doing in your normal state seem perfectly normal when you're manic. The fallout can be catastrophic. Sex might only exist as a fleeting intellectual concept when you're flying high, but you can't explain that to your wife when you come home from a night club at four in the morning, stinking of booze and perfume.

3. Has medication significantly lowered, or affected your sexual drive in any way?

Alastair: I think it's probably lowered my sex drive, really. The medication I take now is primarily to suppress the mania. I was on lithium, originally, which I hated. But since then, I've been prescribed a variety of different drugs, all with pretty much the same intention.

Faye: Why did you hate lithium?

Well, I can remember going for a walk in Colorado, where my sister lived at one time. And I can remember looking at the scenery and knowing that what I was looking at was beautiful. There was a sunset going on and these snow-covered mountains. There was a lake and there were trees. No other man-made thing for miles around. And although I knew that what I was looking at was beautiful, it meant absolutely nothing to me. I felt emotionless. It wasn't beautiful at all. It was nothing.

Adam: That sounds like classic depressive symptoms, doesn't it. No matter what you're shown, or what you experience, you can't take any personal pleasure from it whatsoever.

Alastair: That's right. Part of you is saying, I know this is beautiful, but you're not feeling that.

Faye: And you believe this was due to lithium?

Yes, totally.

Adam: Well, I can't say I've had the same experience with lithium. Although, my experience with it before and after I stopped drinking was totally different, for obvious reasons. Drinking alcohol excessively cancels out the effect of any medication.

But I've often wondered whether lithium can cause sexual dysfunction. Research seems to be inconclusive in this area, particularly as each individual reacts differently. But, in general, I wouldn't say that lithium has affected my sex drive. It's as high now as it ever was since I've changed my lifestyle and improved my health.

So, to recap, I don't believe that medication, per se, has affected my sexual drive. When I say medication, I suppose I'm talking primarily about lithium, rather than all the other psychotherapeutic drugs I've been on over the years.

Chris's View

Increases in, and loss of, libido are common experiences in mania and depression. Risky behaviour and poor impulse control is a common experience with mania and often leads to an increase in sexual partners. This, in turn, leads to relationship break-ups and marital problems that can be hard to resolve. As an individual's mental state improves and insight into past behaviour is realised, guilt feelings are often triggered. Promiscuity can lead to other risks, such as pregnancy, sexually transmitted diseases, and sexual behaviour the person would not normally engage in.

In depression, loss of libido can lead to feelings of guilt, that a significant aspect of a relationship is being unfulfilled. Partners may blame themselves and perceive that there are serious problems within the relationship.

A recent study by Peters et al (2011) concentrated on relapse prevention and barriers that may arise within families. All participants identified benefits of involving relatives in relapse prevention. Some of these benefits included:

» Improved understanding of bipolar disorder
» Relatives gaining a role in illness management
» Improved relationships between each party

When families are included in relapse prevention, the outcome is most often positive. Relationships between clients, their families and care coordinators improve, and family members gain in both experience and confidence. Because of this, the illness is better maintained.

Sexual behaviour (during mania) can be especially problematic. Self-esteem issues often arise, causing guilt and shame for the client and resentment for the family who've been directly affected. Self-esteem issues are often highlighted as a result.

Low self-esteem is not a clinical disorder nor a symptom; it is an element of our personality that is intrinsically human and can vary depending on a range of factors. Self-esteem can be described as, *'a learned, negative, global judgement about the self which, once in place, shapes how the person thinks, feels and behaves on a day-to-day basis* (Melanie Fennell).

Self-esteem is affected by events, development and, of course, our health; bipolar disorder affects how we see ourselves and our perceptions of how people see us.

Lowered self-esteem has been consistently found to occur in several psychiatric disorders, including major depressive disorder, eating disorders, and alcohol and drug abuse. In periods of mania, self-esteem can be inflated, while in depression it can be very low. Living with a diagnosis itself can have a negative impact on self-esteem, so in building your recovery, developing social networks and support around you can help reduce that impact.

Drugs & Alcohol

'I do believe that drugs were the catalyst for
me having my first psychotic episode'

1. How did early experiments with drugs/alcohol affect your mood?

Alastair: My first serious experiment with drugs was when I was at college. This was after I'd been to Epsom, of course. I went to college to do business studies, which I had no real desire to do. My mother had found a place for me and I went along to please her, really. Having disappointed my parents so much up to that point, I thought, okay, I'll go and do this for them. I suppose it was my way of trying to make up for the total balls-up I'd made of my education up until then.

I had a great time at college, I really did. But to me it was all about sex and drugs, pure and simple. I suppose you could say it was like a love affair. I fell in love with drugs – all of them. I'd experimented with cannabis a few times before but this was different. It was available pretty much everywhere, and I smoked it all the time.

My first experience with LSD was also at college, an

experience which was, at times, exceptionally fantastic and at other times terrifying. LSD is one drug that really does alter the state of mind. I believe that everyone should try it at least once in their lives.

Faye: Did this first experience of taking drugs affect your mental state in any way?

I don't think so. Not then. It didn't really affect my moods that much at all. All I know is that LSD certainly changed the way I perceived things. But, having said that, I do believe that drugs were the catalyst for me having my first psychotic episode, before I was ever hospitalised.

Adam: This takes me back to our earlier discussion about adolescence. The time I had my first experience of what I now know to be clinical depression. I began to wonder if it could have been caused by any particular event, my drinking, for instance, that started in my teens. I haven't been able to answer that question successfully. I really don't know. I can't remember taking a drink, and then being plunged into black depression, it didn't work like that. The whole thing was too complex to understand.

I do remember incidents of drinking to excess quite early on, around the age of fourteen or fifteen. The compulsion to drink until I couldn't drink any more. I carried on drinking like that, until I eventually stopped years later.

Drugs were different. There was an element of fear involved that made me wary. Drinking didn't bother me in that respect – even drinking to excess. But I did have a morbid fascination with drugs, even at school, particularly heroin. I remember being obsessed with heroin addicts and drug-addicted rock stars. For some reason, I was drawn to all that stuff, even though it frightened me. Drinking was the safer option – or so I believed – because I knew what I was getting into. A few friends of mine did start to experiment with drugs around the age of fifteen, sixteen, and I tended to avoid them. At least in the early stages.

Faye: What effect did drugs have on you, mentally, when you first tried them?

I don't think I smoked cannabis until I was about sixteen. The effects of that were memorable though, far more unsettling than they were for Alastair. In fact, the experience unhinged me so much I didn't go near it again for a long time. Alcohol tended to lower my mood, or suppress it to some extent, and that, basically, was the affect I was looking for. Anything to calm me down from this anxious, volatile emotional state I seemed to be in most of the time.

What I sought throughout most of my adult life, was anything that would suppress my mood. Downers, barbiturates, sleeping tablets. I loved the effect of these. Drugs like cocaine and speed were too intense. I went through a period of taking speed quite regularly in my twenties, but it tended to put me on edge. My 'fragile' emotional state seemed always on the point of tipping over, like walking a constant tightrope. Even a room full of people could be traumatic. Was I going to veer one way, or the other? That kind of thinking. So I was constantly looking for ways to balance those moods out. As I say, alcohol did it for me for a long time, until even that stopped working.

Faye: My early experiments tended to be with alcohol, too. I did the usual bottle of vodka with friends, that kind of thing, around eighteen or nineteen. I used to drink socially, but at the time I was quite high anyway, so the drinking kind of balanced it out.

When I joined the Navy, I stopped drinking completely. I didn't drink for about fifteen years.

Alastair: You were in the Navy for fifteen years?

Oh no, no! I was in the Navy for about two years, but it didn't work out. After I left, I put my energies into running and the new relationship I had at the time – the man I eventually married. I didn't feel the need to drink. It's only been in the last seven years or so that I've had a real problem with alcohol and found it difficult to stop.

Basically, my marriage broke up, and I was drifting around for a couple of years. Then I ended up seeing this guy who was an alcoholic. He used to go down the pub every night and, of course, I used to go with him. One night, it dawned on me that the drinking was making me feel relaxed, changing my mood and my perceptions. The whole thing really escalated from that point on, even though I hadn't touched alcohol for such a long period prior to that.

Alastair: Well, I indulged in everything right from the start. Alcohol, drugs. Whatever I could get my hands on. But I would say, that people who haven't tried cannabis haven't truly experienced paranoia. Cannabis has a powerful effect on the mind, especially when you first take it. You can experience paranoia in a form that you've never experienced before. And yet the longer you smoke it, and the longer that period is, the more you get away from the paranoia to a less anxious state. I think pretty much everyone who tries cannabis for the first time will have this experience, whereas most people who've never tried drugs will never come close to it. I do believe that.

Adam: Yes, I agree, about cannabis in particular. There's been a lot of argument in the past as to whether cannabis is a dangerous drug – a soft drug, a hard drug etc. They've tried to declassify it and give it a more therapeutic image, and so on. My experience of it is that it taps into an altered state of awareness, in which paranoia is one facet, exactly as you described. At times this can be so complex and overwhelming that you can't seem to find your way out of

4

it – like being in a maze. Then, as you say, you smoke more of it and appear to acclimatise.

But I don't go along with those who say cannabis is a safe drug at all. It's a powerful drug, without a doubt. Mind-altering, and potentially dangerous, especially to anyone with mental health problems.

2. Did you use street drugs as an alternative to prescribed medication?

Faye: I certainly didn't initially. As I said, I tended to use things like running and being in a close relationship to keep me on the level. But recently my drinking has escalated, to the point where I've come to rely on it to balance my moods. I drink when I'm up to bring my mood down, and I drink when I'm down to bring my mood up.

As for street drugs, I don't have much experience. I did try cannabis when I was about eighteen or nineteen, but it didn't really do anything for me. I wasn't interested. Fortunately, I've never been offered anything stronger, because I know I'm prone to addictions. If I tried something stronger, the chances are I'd become addicted to it. So I've always had a steer well clear attitude, which has kept me out of trouble in that respect.

Adam: You felt that drugs were more powerful than alcohol at that point?

Pretty much, yes.

When I was in hospital the last time, there was a girl there who was pregnant and she'd taken LSD, which had completely screwed her up. She was in hospital for about three months trying to get over this one experience. Things like that reaffirmed, for me, the dangers of taking drugs and what they can do to you, physically and mentally. I suppose I dreaded ending up like that, having already had my share of anxiety and depression.

Alastair: Well, I believe very much that the first psychotic episode I had, which was in Los Angeles, was down to drugs. I do like my anagrams – as Adam will tell you. L.A. is my name Al backwards. I saw this as a sign, that I'd been put there for some divine purpose, and started behaving irrationally. Looking back, I see that incident as my first mad episode, where I was actually physically forced onto an aeroplane and sent home.

Faye: As a direct result of taking drugs?

Well, yes, to an extent. But there was another big influential point in my life which we haven't yet discussed, which I think is where it all began. This was the actual catalyst for me becoming bipolar. The airport incident wasn't the first instance of mania, but was probably the most significant in terms of severity. The incident I'm about to tell you about was, I believe, the thing that caused it.

Adam: That's interesting that you can identify one particular cause.

Absolutely.

At the time, I was working in London, selling insurance and investment advice to doctors. My boss there was a very good friend of mine, and probably the most intelligent person I'd ever met in my life. He had this photographic memory and could actually recall the date and time of discussions we'd had months ago. He was amazing. I suppose you could say I almost hero-worshipped him, really.

Then one night, inexplicably, he blew his brains out at his girlfriend's. She actually found him in her cellar, still conscious. She called the paramedics and he died on the way to hospital.

'A few friends of mine did start to experiment with drugs around the age of fifteen, sixteen, and I tended to avoid them. At least in the early stages.'

Faye: God, that must have been horrendous.

Yes, it really was dreadful.

A couple of weeks after, she asked me if I could stay at hers to look after her cats, while she went away for a few days. As she'd been a very good friend of mine, I agreed. So my girlfriend and me went round to her flat, the same place where the incident had occurred, and settled in for the night. I later found out that the bed we were sleeping in was in fact my deceased friend's, but I didn't know that at the time. Anyway, we settled down and everything was fine. I hadn't drunk anything that night, or taken any drugs, so I was quite rational. Compus mentis, as they say.

I woke up at about three o'clock in the morning, aware of something coming up the stairs. A kind of energy, or force of some sort. I can remember thinking, okay, I can really feel this energy but I'm not going to be afraid.

Adam: What kind of force – malicious?

Not really, I just felt an energy. I didn't know what it was, I'd never experienced anything like it before in my life. Like most other people, I'd pooh-poohed all that stuff. Spirits and ghosts and all that. But I knew there was something, an energy, a force, coming up the stairs. I just felt instinctively that it was my friend, that this was his force, his spirit, his energy. I can remember saying to myself, I am totally open to this, I have nothing to fear.

Then I felt this force arrive at the bottom of my feet and, like electricity, it slowly moved up, through my feet, my calves, my legs. I kept saying to myself, I am totally open to this, I am totally open.

Then, as I lay there in the bed, I felt a huge pain in my face and what felt like blood dripping down my cheeks. At this point, I was terrified. I couldn't move. I shouted out to my girlfriend 'Put the light on!' Then, I sat bolt upright, and this force threw me from the edge of the bed against the wall – four feet away.

Adam: That must have been a truly terrifying experience. But a lot of people would say it was a hallucination caused by drugs you'd taken before, or even the trauma of losing your friend.

To me it was a hundred-percent real. It wasn't delusional, or imagined in any way.

After that, I went to see a medium at a place called the College of Psychics – who were, apparently, the most reputable body in London. And without knowing who the hell I was, this woman described nearly everything that happened. She even used expressions my friend used to use, things she can't possibly have known about.

Adam: That really is an amazing story. I've certainly never had an experience like that. But I have had experiences similar to the ones you described, where I've felt a deep peace come over me for no apparent reason. These were isolated incidents, and not something I'd put down to the supernatural.

Giving up drugs and alcohol has led me to question many of the views I held and to seek answers elsewhere. I even went to an astrologer once, who told me that certain people are born with an innate sensitivity to drugs and alcohol. I put myself in this category, without a doubt. Taking drugs and drinking alcohol does something to me that it doesn't do to other people. My chemical make-up is such that I need to avoid these combinations at all costs if I want to stay well. It's the tightrope syndrome. How far do you push before the experiment goes wrong? Take too much of this or too much of that and, bang! down you go.

I've learned in the last few years of being sober and off any mind-altering drugs that abstinence is definitely the best state for me to be in. By far the safest way.

3. How much do you think your psychotic episodes were influenced by drugs/alcohol?

Faye: All through my worst years, my suicidal years, as I call them, I wasn't drinking. All the self-harming and the suicide attempts happened before I started drinking, so I suppose it was something of a refuge, an escape. I'd think, right, I'm not going to hurt myself, I'm just going to drink. For a while that seemed to work, but it's hard to get the balance right without tipping over.

Adam: So it's the refuge of one extreme to another?

Yes, I think so. As I said before, I wasn't using drugs to any great extent, so I can't say that they had any influence on my moods at the time. But the drinking helped with those feelings of being out of control. That became my way of coping.

The issues I had around food at the time also influenced my moods. By controlling my weight, I was also, to some extent, controlling the way I felt. Looking back, I can see that all these elements made it harder for me to stay on an even keel for long. The tightrope syndrome, as you called it.

Alastair: This is an interesting question. Mania, to those who haven't experienced it, has to be one of the most profound mental states that there is. What you have, during mania, is an effect that, under normal circumstances, only powerful drugs would achieve. And, of course, there are certain drugs that come close to inducing this mental state, but nothing can actually top it as a peak experience.

Now, I've got two children. Every father should say that the happiest day of his life is the day his children are born, right? Well, castigate me if you will, because it sounds awful, but the happiest day of my life was the day I took my first ecstasy pill. I know that's a horrible thing to admit, but it's true. I think it's fair to say that I felt better on that pill than I do when I'm totally manic. I felt fantastic. I thought, oh, my God! The World is going to change. We're going to abolish war. We're going to abolish poverty. We're going to abolish greed, and all these awful things human nature has inflicted on us. All through this one drug – MDMA.

Adam: Ecstasy had a profound effect on me, too. I didn't take a huge quantity, like some people, but I took enough to feel all those feelings you've described. But again, for me, it was always the consequence of taking these mind-altering substances and what it did to me later. The comedown took a long time to get over. With ecstasy, in particular, you're still lying awake at four in the morning, if you get to bed at all. Then there's the orchestra still playing in your head, as if you've taken the nightclub home with you! Any benefits I got from taking the drug were always offset by the comedown. My head became a barren wasteland for days after.

Faye: I suppose, for me, psychosis is associated more with the depressive phase. I've never been sectioned while I was manic, for instance. Plus, I've never experimented with hallucinogenic drugs like ecstasy and LSD, so I can't say these might have been a contributory factor in me being diagnosed bipolar.

But there are varying degrees of psychosis, aren't there. I suppose it depends on your interpretation of the word. I certainly know what it's like to be delusional, and to have mad ideas that seem to come from nowhere.

Alastair: Well I've certainly experienced psychosis as a direct result of taking drugs. But then I've also become psychotic without taking anything at all. Perhaps that's the true definition of manic depression, that it can manifest of its own accord without needing any particular trigger.

Chris's View

For people with bipolar disorder, there are no beneficial effects from illicit drug taking. The range of so called 'legal highs' also have a detrimental effect on the person's health. It is far safer not to use any substance that can cause changes in mood or trigger psychotic experiences.

Some of the comments from those I've worked with range from, 'Yes, but drugs are everywhere,' to, 'My friends use them so why can't I?'

The simple truth is – their risks. There is no supporting evidence that illicit drugs, such as cannabis, cocaine, and amphetamines can relieve mental illness. In fact, the opposite is true – particularly on a long-term basis.

Below are some reasons not to use illicit drugs (including alcohol):

» Alcohol acts as a depressant upon the nervous system and can exacerbate depressive symptoms
» Drugs like cocaine and 'speed' can accelerate the manic phase, triggering either psychosis, or the depressive phase that follows
» Diuretic effects of alcohol will effect lithium levels

The negative interactions with prescribed medication can also add problems. The sedating nature of alcohol, for instance, will prohibit any medications that could have a sedative side-effect. Prescribed medications can also be abused. Benzodiazepines (temazepam, valium), when used with alcohol, produce a lethargic, heavily sedated response that slows reactions.

Alcohol is often used by those with bipolar disorder to help relieve mood swings. Because of its addictive qualities and the consequences for long-term physical and mental health, it is rarely advisable.

Below are some of the reasons alcohol is abused:

» Facilitate social networking
» Reduce anxiety
» Aid sleep
» 'Knock out' the effects of feeling slightly manic

Keep a diary of the amount you drink and try to cut down when necessary. Any recurrent problems with alcohol may be treated separately by consulting a doctor or healthcare worker.

Think about actually *doing* things differently. Write down all the reasons you want to stay dry/clean – make copies and carry one around with you. Alcohol or drug use filled a great deal of your time, so do invest time in finding ways to manage without them.

Do identify your triggers and trigger situations that might make you more likely to drink; think about your routine, places you go and who you meet. What is likely to happen if you go to certain places, or meet certain people?

Do use support groups like Alcoholics Anonymous (AA), Narcotics Anonymous (NA), or other groups that offer help.

A Substance Use Diary is a very effective and simple tool to clarify exactly how much you're drinking/using – and the amount of money you're spending!

Once your substance use is under control, consider getting support with some of the issues that may have led you to rely on them. These can include:

» Depression
» Anxiety
» Mania
» Anger
» Sleep problems

Think about the positive consequences to your health, your finances, and your relationships that will result from the changes you're making. You'll have the ability to think more clearly and to manage life's problems. You'll be much better able to manage your illness.

Write positive, encouraging statements down to help you keep focused on what it is you want to achieve. Be realistic. Think about each day and try not to convince yourself that the job is done. Celebrate your goals and achievements, however small.

Creativity

'The other important factor is that I'm
absolutely driven in everything I do'

1. Do you consider yourself a creative, or practical person?

Alastair: I'm more creative than I am practical. Although now, at this stage of my life, I'm actually very, very lazy and don't see myself as being creative at all. But one thing I do like, that's fascinated me for years, is anagrams, mixing words around to make strange meanings. When I'm high – that's manic, rather than on drugs – I always get this obsession with words in all their forms. That's when I feel I'm most creative. When it comes to things like painting, or writing, I'd have to say no, not really.

But I will stress again that I'm desperately lazy, and that's been an ongoing feature of my illness throughout the years. That's one of the worst aspects of depression. The lowering of mood and general blunting of the senses. That awful lack of enthusiasm that seems to pervade everything you do.

Adam: I've always been highly creative, right from an early age. My dad used to bring home rolls of paper for me to draw on. He'd cut them up with scissors and lay them out on the table, and I'd be away for hours, totally engrossed in the moment. I loved to sketch characters from my imagination, faces in particular. One of my dad's friends was an artist in London. He'd worked with another artist, Richard Williams, who'd done a lot of film work. Anyway, my dad showed him something I'd drawn and he thought it was brilliant, highly original for a child that age. Of course, my dad liked to remind me of this years later when I'd stopped drawing altogether.

So, yes, I did have certain talents in the artistic field from a young age. My Art teacher at secondary school told my parents they should get me into Art college as soon as possible. The same with English. A teacher at my junior school told a friend of my mum that I was an author in the making. Creative Writing was my favourite subject, something I excelled at. But when I left school, I had no ambition. None whatsoever.

My creative talents actually frightened me to be honest. I felt different, vulnerable in some way. All the other kids around me tended to excel at things like sport and fighting and I didn't. My mum has a photo of me taken around that time, looking very angelic, with this mop of blonde hair. I looked a bit like Brian Jones from The Rolling Stones. Ironically, he was plagued with mental problems, too.

Faye: I'm definitely creative, but I'm also very practical, a mixture of the two really. The other important factor is that I'm absolutely driven in everything I do. I have to be the best that I can be. I worked in a factory once, making contact lenses, and I was the top performing employee on the site. The company loved me and were upset when I left, but that's the way I am. Everything I do is a hundred percent, and because of that, I tend to get frustrated.

But I've definitely got both traits, the practicality and

the creativity. I love cooking, for instance, and I do a lot of crafts. Obviously, I've got my writing as well, which gives me a great deal of pleasure.

Also, I have a scientific background. My first job was working in a laboratory. I loved that process, following instructions that lead to a conclusion of some sort. The gathering of research and finding all these obscure details.

Adam: Did this follow on from your academic qualifications at school?

Yes, it did. I was good at everything. The school swot, as I said before. I got nine As and a B for my GCSEs, and the B was for Art, which I was expecting to fail. So, yes, I was an overachiever, definitely. But the downside of that is I make myself ill. I push myself so hard that eventually I come crashing down. It's a real double-edged sword.

I've done quite a few Open University courses, and you always have deadlines for submitting your assignments. My partner will often say to me, 'Right, that's it! You're going to send that one now. You're doing no more work on it, it's finished!' And he would physically send my work for me. Otherwise, I would tear it to pieces, because I'm so driven to perfection.

Alastair: You've just reminded me of something that I loved doing. Although, I said that I wasn't very good at English, I did have a talent for poetry. I remember one time, I'd written a poem at Epsom, and the teacher couldn't believe I'd actually written it. He was convinced I'd stolen it from someone else and made me prove that I hadn't.

Faye: Why didn't he believe it was yours?

Because of my appalling track record academically. In the end he accepted that it was mine and gave me thirty out of thirty. This was as much a surprise to me as it was to him, as I usually didn't do very well at this sort of subject at all.

Adam: You had an obvious talent there that you didn't build on. This was the same for me when I left school. I deliberately went against my parents wishes. Refused to go to Art school, refused to look for a job. All I wanted to do was go down the beach and laze around with my mates, doing exactly as I wanted. Any natural creativity I had was wasted.

Right through school, I'd always been involved in music. In fact, that's been a constant interest right through my life, being in bands and duos, and meeting other musicians. Often things didn't get past the rehearsal stage, but I loved that environment, the thrill of creating something musically. Even when I was in a band and we were playing gigs, I still preferred the intimacy of rehearsal. I was never really comfortable playing in front of a crowd, and even turned down a job offer to sing with a semi-professional band when I was younger because I was too nervous. I was the classic bedroom player. More comfortable sitting round writing songs with another guitarist and a tape recorder. That was what I enjoyed the most.

2. How have the extremes of both mania and depression affected your creativity?

Alastair: I feel very creative in my head when I'm in a manic phase. Everything seems to have meaning. Even ordinary objects you wouldn't think twice about. But when I'm depressed, or flat, which I would say is a fair percentage of the time, it's nothing, my mind is more or less blank. A kind of creative deadness, if that makes sense.

Adam: I used to believe that mania affected my creativity, in that it enabled me to produce more work, to be even more creative. Being manic, I would have all these crazy

'So, yes, I was
an overachiever,
definitely. But the
downside of that is
I make myself ill. I
push myself so hard
that eventually I come
crashing down. It's
a real double-edged
sword.'

ideas. I bought a PA system and a microphone once, took it home and set it up in the front room. After a few drinks, there I was, in my perfect environment, a kind of fantasy land with me in the starring role – and no audience! But in that feverish state you don't need anyone. You're totally self-sufficient – and totally deluded as well.

Mania and creativity are interlinked. It's so easy to make yourself believe that in that state you can create more, that your field of perception has opened up to a higher degree. But, unfortunately, all that manic energy tends to burn itself out quickly. All these great ideas you have are lost in the flurry of activity. You haven't got the time to set them down.

It's the same with writing. You're in this incredibly productive manic state, getting all these wonderfully inspired words down. Then you come back later to revise what you've written and find that it's rubbish.

I always think of the Jack Nicholson character in *The Shining*, pounding the keys with that deranged look. That's me when I'm manic!

Faye: You don't think there are any benefits in this respect, then?

Well, at least with mania there's a certain amount of creativity, even if it does burn out quickly. With depression there's just deadness, as Alastair calls it. There's no creativity at all. It's an ongoing struggle, a kind of survival where all your senses are shut down. Every move you make is tortuous, from getting out of bed to answering the door to the postman.

Faye: Yes, depression is the worst. In depression you can't do anything. You just completely switch off and hide yourself away from everything. Then you get the highs, the mania, and everything's fantastic.

But, like you, I find that the mania affects my ability to create. It's like your head's going to explode. You've got all these ideas coming at you and nowhere to go with them.

Alastair: You're bombarded with ideas, one after another.

Exactly. If you could find a way to contain all that energy it would be great. But you can't. It's like a whirlpool spinning you round and round. You can't really make sense of anything, even if you think you can. And God knows what these ideas must sound like to other people when you try to express them. They just think you're mad, which, of course, at the time you are.

Alastair: Absolutely. The complete opposite to depression, where everything is an effort. When you're manic, you go with the flow. This is when I tend to use the anagrams. The words just come flying at me, and I twist them around until they make sense. So, in spite of all the mad stuff going on, I think you're actually very creative when you're manic. You certainly believe you are.

Adam: That's another common facet of mania, this fascination for words and anagrams. It was certainly one of mine, although not on quite the same scale you used to take it. But I did used to become obsessed with car number plates and billboards, flyers in shop windows and that kind of thing. The most obscure detail would have a major significance when I was in that state.

But I know you took it a step further. The anagrams became a much more dominant feature in your manic state.

Alastair: Well, yes they did, but not initially. I think it came about when I started looking at my name. You know. What it meant and what it looked like when I'd rearranged the letters. Then later it did become a far stronger feature. It actually took over and became obsessive. Everything I read and saw on the TV would have some huge significance, like coded messages from the cosmos that only I could interpret. It used to drive all my friends and my family mad, but to me it was perfectly normal to think like that. After all, I was a super being, wasn't I!

So while I wouldn't say that I'm a particularly creative person ordinarily, I can be when I'm busy. During that time I'm filled with ideas and things. It's impossible to stop them.

3. Do you believe that medication, such as lithium, blunts creativity?

Faye: I can't say that I've noticed. I've been on lithium now for about eight years and, to be honest, I haven't really noticed much of an effect at all. I know Alastair mentioned seeing a beautiful sunset in Colorado and feeling nothing. I've been like that, too, but I don't believe it was caused by medication. More likely the general apathy you feel in depression.

I still get the ups and downs, the same shifts in mood.

Adam: To the same extent?

It's hard to say because I tend to drink a lot more now. I would need to do a period of, say, a few months, where I'm not doing anything but taking the medication. See how I get on with that and assess the changes, if there were any.

But I would say that I'm pretty much as creative now as I used to be. I know they say that lithium blunts creativity, and a lot of writers and artists have said this over the years, but I haven't experienced that personally. It isn't a particularly extreme medication that overwhelms you, or distorts your thinking. It's more a softly-softly drug that you barely realise you're on.

When I'm feeling okay, I still get plenty of ideas and inspiration.

Alastair: Well I couldn't stand lithium. I really couldn't. It's such a deadening drug, like a blanket someone's thrown over your senses. You don't feel any emotion when you're on lithium. Everything is a chore. You can look at something beautiful and it means absolutely nothing to you. I really meant it when I said that. In depression you have some feelings, even if they're mostly unpleasant. With lithium, you're cut off from feeling anything at all.

The reason they gave me lithium in the first place was to stop me having a manic episode. To make sure that did not happen. And yet, without the manic episode, it's almost as if you have nothing to really look forward to. So I think the lithium and the depression do work together, but in a negative way.

Adam: Having been on lithium now for over ten years, I can't say I've experienced that deadening effect you talk about. When I was drinking and taking drugs, generally going off the rails, I wasn't able to do anything. Writing. Music. All that burned out in the end because of my extreme mood swings and self-destructive behaviour. It stopped me from finishing anything. Being on lithium and changing my lifestyle has enabled me to recapture that focus. I can finish whatever I happen to be working on instead of burning out all the time. An extreme mood swing now, in either mania or depression, would be catastrophic in terms of production, not to mention the cost to my physical and mental wellbeing.

Alastair: But you have to acknowledge the role of drugs in creativity, don't you? Cannabis, for instance. I often feel more creative when I've smoked a couple of joints. Ecstasy is another one. Certain chemicals have an incredibly powerful influence over the mind.

I don't know if you'd relate it to creativity, but dancing was one of my favourite things in the whole wide world. Dancing meant everything to me. The reason I'd go to a club, wasn't to meet women or anything, it would be purely to experience music through my body. And that's what I lived for in my earlier years. But I don't know. Would you call that creativity?

Faye: Well, yes, I would. Anything that inspires you really. People tend to think of it in terms of art and literature, but it covers so many different areas. Anything you apply to your thoughts, inspirations, and dreams. That's creativity.

Chris's View

People with bipolar disorder often tell me they are more creative when 'high'. They claim much of their best work is done during these times. These periods of increased energy and greater productivity are often missed by the individual who claims he can't produce anything without them.

In her book, *Touched by Fire,* Kay Jamison discusses the link between creativity and bipolar disorder. In this, she makes clear that new or creative ideas don't come solely from periods of manic or elevated mood. Many of those diagnosed dismiss the 'cosh' effect of medication and refuse to take it, claiming it dampens their natural creative drives. This can lead to alcohol or illicit substance abuse in an attempt to recreate the original intensity of feeling.

Sometimes, having a mental illness such as bipolar can mean reduced employment opportunities. Low income, poverty and reduced quality of life all make the risk of relapse more likely. But this needn't equate with giving up. A mood diary or reflective log can help establish patterns in maladaptive thinking. Simply scoring or rating mood on a daily basis can pinpoint problem areas and help in recovery.

Cognitive therapy can help towards removing dysfunctional beliefs. Underlying assumptions we may have formed about ourselves, based on experiences early in life, can become core beliefs that come to dominate our thinking. A sense of hopelessness and poor self-esteem are commonly experienced and can be heightened by inactivity.

Setting goals that are realistic and achievable can help reduce stress and assist in motivation. This can then lead to increased control over thoughts, behaviours and outcomes.

Mania

'Nothing at all can stop you and nothing can get in your way. It's the ultimate delusional fantasy'

1. When was your first episode of mania?

Alastair: I suppose my first episode of mania was about twenty years ago in Los Angeles where I'd been living for a couple of years. I'd been smoking this strong cannabis every day and not looking after my diet all that well. I'm also a diabetic, so any extremes in my mood tend to be quite debilitating. I actually stopped taking insulin for about a week, and I stopped eating. So I don't know if my first psychotic episode was linked to my diabetes or because of the cannabis – or if it was just the natural onset of bipolar.

Around this time I became convinced that I was the Chosen One – a saviour of some sort. I'd go from feeling I was Jesus, or God, to feeling I was the Devil. Sometimes an amalgam of them all. I was absolutely convinced of it. And in this state, I believed that if I didn't eat, I didn't need to take insulin. There was this, sort of, mad logic underpinning it all.

But I really lost it out there in L.A. So much so that

my sister actually got me on a flight back to England. They nearly didn't let me on the plane. I can remember thinking, ah – the world has finally realised I'm here! I'm going to be flown off to Richard Branson's island where there'll be fifty virgins waiting for me. I'll be recognised as the Messiah, the Chosen One.

Then I arrived back in England thinking, what the hell am I doing here? I hate this country. I left it a few years ago with no desire to ever come back. I was furious and completely unhinged. So what did I do? Well, I did what any normal person would have done under the circumstances. I jumped on the luggage carousel at Heathrow Airport and started dancing like a madman!

Faye: No medical intervention in America prior to that?

No, but it was my first major manic episode. So, after dancing on this luggage carousel, I remember seeing this policeman and marching straight up to him and saying, 'Look – all I want is a f ---- spliff!' Luckily my father turned up. He'd been notified by my sister to meet me at Heathrow. Now my father's a doctor and he was able to reason with the policeman to stop me being arrested. But by then I was incensed, enraged at the world for ignoring me. Here I was, the Messiah, the Chosen One, this gift to mankind everyone's been waiting for, and the bastards are treating me like a criminal.

Faye: I had my first episode of mania about the age of nineteen or twenty. At the time I was in a long-term relationship and I had this, kind of, brainstorm. I suddenly gave up smoking, took up running, quit my job, left my boyfriend and joined the navy – all in the space of a couple of months! None of this was picked up at the time. It's only now, looking back, that I can see I was sky high. Completely off the wall.

Alastair: You joined the Navy while you were manic?

Oh yes. They sent me for a psychiatric assessment because I'd had depression before, and because of my dad's history. And the psychiatrist said, 'Oh well, there's absolutely nothing wrong with you then, is there.' Two years later, that same psychiatrist had to discharge me from the Navy with depression, and he said, 'Well, clearly I got it wrong then, didn't I.'

So, yes, that was quite a turbulent period in my life and my first experience of how powerful bipolar can be. The idea that I could change my entire life on a whim and do anything I wanted to without any thought behind it at all. I suppose it goes back to some of our earlier discussions about being delusional.

Adam: I can't remember exactly what triggered my first episode, but by this stage I was already way out of control. My behaviour at home got worse. I'd be sat at home listening to music on headphones, my wife and son in bed, and I'd suddenly decide to just get up and go. I'd end up wandering the streets for miles like a vagrant. At one point, I became so delusional I thought I was this big, rich rock star. I'd stroll around town wearing a leather waistcoat, with long, blonde hair and two gold earrings, convinced I was the lost member of Guns 'n' Roses or the Rolling Stones.

My first section under the Mental Health Act was in 1992. I was actually taken off the streets because of my diminished mental state. This led to a period of time spent in a psychiatric hospital where I was treated with a combination of drugs and gradually brought down. This led, inevitably, to the black depressions that always followed the massive highs. The only way I can describe it is like coming down onto a runway and realising the plane's run out of fuel. That's it. Finished. This incredible adventure you've been on for the past few days, or weeks, is over. You're plunged back into cold, hard reality.

2. Can you describe some of your thoughts and perceptions during this heightened state?

Alastair: Well, you believe – to use that phrase you coined earlier – that you're a super-being. Nothing at all can stop you and nothing can get in your way. It's the ultimate delusional fantasy. You're bigger than the universe. Bigger than God even.

Adam: And normal life seems so utterly trivial, doesn't it. You walk into a shop and see a queue forming and it raises your blood pressure instantly. Super-beings don't wait in queues, do they! They need to be at the front, being served quickly so they can move on to their next peak experience. There's this incredible sense of urgency about everything you do. A constant seeking of experience to escape the boring and the mundane.

In some ways, mania forces you to live in the present moment, because of its heightened sense of arousal. You're so aware of this huge energy current going through you, that you can't bear anything to interrupt it. The flow of thoughts you're having, and the excitement generated by them, is all that matters.

Faye: And the feeling that everyone's about three steps behind you all the time!

Adam: Yes, that constant irritation with people, that they just don't realise what you're trying to achieve. Simple things, like someone asking you where you're going, or engaging you in some pointless conversation. They simply can't keep up with you. Your thinking speeds up. You have this cascade of ideas that all merge into one.

'I really lost it out there in L.A. So much so that my sister actually got me on a flight back to England.'

Faye: I can do anything when I'm in this state. I'm absolutely invincible. Whatever I want to achieve, I can do it. I'll do whatever I can to get to where I want to be and I won't let anyone stop me.

When I joined the Navy I was going to be the first female Admiral. I was going all the way! The incredible confidence I felt got me through basic training because I was so high and had such energy.

This initial period of mania lasted on and off for about a year, but I wasn't actually diagnosed with bipolar until I was thirty. One of the reasons I wasn't diagnosed earlier was the fact that I had a lot of different doctors. The longest I'd seen any one consultant had been about a year. They kept changing, so I wasn't able to build up a relationship with any of them. Consequently there was a lot I wasn't telling them. Looking back, it's easy to see what was happening, but at the time I felt so fantastic I thought, please, just let me get on with it.

Alastair: Yes, you do become extremely delusional. I'd often be convinced that people knew all about me, that there was this big conspiracy going on. 'There he is!' they'd say. 'There's Allah! We know it's him, but he wants to be left alone.' I'd be playing it cool at the bar, going along with the whole thing. But again, there was this supreme confidence that went with all my actions. Everyone would be talking about me, pointing at me. You feel like a celebrity, a superstar. The most important being that ever walked the earth.

Adam: It's the thinking that characterises mania. Imagine the most confident person on earth and times that by ten. That's the power of the manic state. Looking back, I'm amazed at how I survived some of the situations I got myself in. I was a one man army, a force of nature. People moved out of my way when they saw me coming, such was the aura that surrounded me. And I don't mean that in a boastful sense, either.

Ultimately, that's what happens. You become so detached from reality that people avoid you completely. Even your friends and your family see you as a threat, a complete nuisance. It's one of the most alienating and self-destructive conditions of all.

Faye: Did you ever become violent or abusive?

In the later stages, yes, I did. Although I didn't physically assault anyone, I did become threatening and verbally abusive on a number of occasions. At one point, during a spell in a psychiatric unit, I had to be restrained by members of staff for threatening one of them with a pool cue. I was out of control, beyond reasoning.

Conversely, I can still recall some of the more amazing flights of fantasy that came over me during these phases. I think it was Abbie Hoffman who said that no drug in the world comes close to the heights you reach during mania, and I can attest to this. From my waking moments (if I got any sleep at all), I lived in this bizarre parallel universe, with me in the starring role. I was the King, the Lord of the Manor, the Prince Regent, whatever you want to call it. And whatever I said had to be done, or else! Fantastic for the time it lasted, but not so good when you're forced to come down.

3. What, if any, are the benefits of being in this state?

Alastair: One of the benefits is your complete indifference to most things. Things society claims to be so important, like politics and money. When you're manic, you don't care about money. It's just there to service whatever it is you happen to be doing at the time. Generosity would come naturally to me. I'd often buy people drinks in the pub, thinking the money was in my bank account. The desire to live life to the very full, but on my terms. In mania, this is often translated as doing exactly what you want to do to the exclusion of all else. You have this enormous energy that's physical, not just mental, in its hold over you. You feel god-like and supreme, that you don't have to fit in with society's perceptions of right and wrong. Normal means boring, something beneath you.

Faye: I'm not sure about benefits, but I suppose it goes back to the basic feelings of being highly confident. Of course, there's the dangerous element, too, as we talked about before, regarding things like sexual behaviour and money. There are positives in terms of how much you can get done, progress towards your goals etc. But there's always that fear at the back of your mind that it isn't going to last.

I suppose I'm grateful I didn't have yours or Adam's experience, in terms of the psychotic nature of the illness. I never attacked anyone, or became violent in any way. But if you look at my achievements over the years, you can see where being high has pushed me into doing things I might not have attempted otherwise. Running marathons, travelling, seeking relationships. On the face of it these are positive things that ordinary people aspire to, but there's always a price to pay when you've achieved them through burnout.

I wouldn't say I'm a horrible person when I'm depressed, but there are certainly more benefits to being high. You know, generally having more go and being happier rather than the constant introspection of being down. I often fantasise what it would be like to have unlimited energy. To tap into that highly creative state all the time. You get close to it during mania, but it's hard to hang on to for any length of time.

Adam: Then you go from being 'happy' to being out of control.

I have been out of control, yes, but mainly in my head. I've never been hospitalised for mania, only depression. Although it has been threatened in the last six months, where the doctors have been keeping an eye on my moods and tinkering with my medication levels. My partner keeps an eye on me and makes sure I don't go completely off the wall. The whole thing's a kind of balancing act really. But I'm getting better, learning to read the signs. If I'm up at one, two in the morning, I know something's going wrong. Once my normal patterns of behaviour change it's never a good sign. I think that's what you have to do in the end. Keep an eye on yourself, be vigilant and look for the signs.

Adam: The energy that goes with the manic phase is really quite incredible. That's something I'd not looked at before. The way you perceive things. That sense that ordinary or mundane living is almost beneath you. As Alastair said, you're just not concerned with the things people usually concern themselves with. You don't have the same worries, the same preoccupations. Why would you worry about an income when you're already a multi-millionaire! It's that kind of thinking that separates you from all those poor, ordinary mortals on the earth plane.

When I was manic – right up there on the top of that rollercoaster, money was there for me to use and abuse at leisure, whether it was mine or somebody else's. I would always have a constant source available – or at least I did in my mind. It was like all the money in the world belonged to me and all I had to do was ask for it. Quite simple really. Delusional, but simple.

Alastair: And another thing I would say about that state, which can be an advantage but can also be dangerous, is that you're totally fearless. You're not scared of anyone or anything. If anyone gives you a bad look, you'll be at their throats immediately. Again, it's the super-being business. In your own mind you're totally in control.

Faye: And this can lead you into dangerous situations.

Oh, absolutely.

One of the most dangerous things I ever did was during a manic episode. I was living in Shepherd's Bush at the time, which was like a little microcosm of the World. There were Arabs, Jews, Chinese people, black people. It was a multi-mix of races and cultures, and everyone seemed to get on.

One day, I noticed all these posters going up. Little polystyrene posters, a bit smaller than A4 size paper. The header said '10,000 Man March'. Everyone knew that this was the Nation of Islam wanting to have a march, similar to the one they had in the States which they called the 'Million Man March'. Anyway, these posters were everywhere. Tied to lampposts, stuck to the walls. Absolutely everywhere.

Now, I got really irritated by this. I imagined that these racist black people were planning some huge event. I was appalled, as two of my best friends at the time were black guys.

Adam: And you believed you needed to intervene?

That's right. As you know, in the manic phase all your emotions are heightened. You can feel extreme happiness and extreme anger, almost in the same breath. So I decided I was going to have a little word with the Nation of Islam immediately.

Off I went to the Goldhawk Road, where I knew they had an office, or meeting point there, and demanded to speak to someone. They said come back in for an appointment and gave me a date for a few days later. Now I'd been dwelling on all this and turning it over in my mind, thinking how dare these people do such a thing. As I said, I can't abide racism of any description. I remember grabbing one of their posters, going home, and writing on the back 'One White Devil-Man Walk' – which I spelt – W.A.R.K.K.K. Then, bare-chested and wearing an open leather jacket, I marched off towards the Nation of Islam's HQ, with this sign tied round my neck.

Along the way, I started pointing out the sign to passers-by. Every poster I saw I would rip down, either with my hands or my teeth. I was walking in the middle of the road, being quite brazen about the whole thing.

Faye: Did the police intervene?

No, I don't believe I saw any police presence at that point. Bearing in mind, this was before the official March itself. Anyway, I remember banging on their doors and they let me in. Three tall, very elegant-looking black guys, all suited, with shaved heads. One of them reached out to move me towards the door and I just screamed 'Don't touch me!' He really wanted me to move outside because the place was absolutely packed, which infuriated me even more. They had these little TVs on, obviously showing videos of Louis Farrakhan, the leader of the Nation of Islam in the States. And there were all these little black kids in there watching. There must have been around thirty people in there at least.

Eventually, they got me outside where I screamed at them, 'How can you hate me for the colour of my skin! We are all human beings!' and all the rest of it. They just ignored me and closed the door, so I ended up banging on the window, screaming at the top of my voice, 'I am Satan!'

Then I just walked away. People in the street would move quickly when they saw me coming along. I was walking through the traffic, not caring about the cars or the danger. People would look away, not daring to look me in the eyes. How I didn't get arrested is beyond me.

Faye: That's incredible. I'm amazed you're still alive.

Well that's the astonishing thing about it. It's almost as if people recognise how disturbed you are and back off. There is, after all, something quite disconcerting about one man behaving in such a way with complete disregard for his own safety.

Adam: I've had similar incidents to that. Not quite on the scale of Alastair's one-man protest against the Nation of Islam, but I've come close. For some reason during mania, all fear is removed. Again, it's that delusional state that's so common in manic depression. I'm sure it affects people differently in the way that it manifests, but it's a recognised feature of the illness.

What's interesting to me is the way it completely takes over, creating a kind of monstrous alter-ego. You take on these wild personas and become someone else.

During one manic episode, I saw a customised motorbike in a magazine. The owner lived in Swindon and wanted around three thousand pounds for it. I was unemployed at the time but that didn't stop me. Off I went to the building society to get a loan and within twenty minutes had three thousand pounds transferred into my account. Fantastic! I phoned the guy in Swindon, hired a van and drove up there right away. He turned out to be this very amenable Hells Angel type with photos of bikes he'd built on the kitchen wall. We drank coffee and chatted for a bit, then drove to this lock-up in Swindon, and there was this beautiful, customised motorbike I'd seen in the magazine. He wanted one last go on it and roared off up the road with no helmet on, which I thought was incredibly cool. Then we loaded the bike into the back of the hired van, strapped it to the sides and I drove home.

Another time, I walked into an estate agents in Canford Cliffs, and asked to look at one of the million-pound houses I'd seen in the window. I told the sales girl I was a musician, waiting to catch a flight back to L.A. She must have believed me, because she got on the phone straight away and booked a viewing for later that afternoon! Of course, I didn't turn up. By then I'd found something better to do.

Chris's View

Identifying changes in the daily life of the service user is a powerful and effective tool to avoid relapse. Morris (2004) identifies the following as symptoms that can lead to a manic episode.

- » Euphoria
- » Ideas flowing too fast
- » Difficulty concentrating
- » Delusions (psychosis)
- » Rapid speech
- » Feeling creative
- » Feeling irritable
- » Spending money more freely
- » Decreased need for sleep
- » Energetic/very active
- » Feeling very important
- » Heavy drinking of alcohol
- » Taking street drugs
- » Increased sex drive

If you re-read the above, you can identify many of the experiences that Faye, Alastair and Adam talk about.

The Early Warning Signs (EWS) are individual to the service user, and can be identified in order to aid those closest in giving support. Most frequently reported are sleeping less, increased sociability and racing thoughts. Identifying these signs enables family members, or care coordinators to intervene, thus reducing the impact for the service user. The relapse period tends to last on average 20-28 days.

Mania often requires inpatient care to manage risk and allow treatment. This can sometimes require compulsory admission (as in the case of Adam and Alastair), whenever the patient is deemed to be out of control or irrational. Highly disturbed behaviour may need to be acutely treated with anti-psychotics or benzodiazepines – or both (rapid tranquillisation). Excess stimulation is best avoided and as calm an atmosphere as possible provided. Milder degrees of mania may be treated with intensive community support from specialist services.

The first step is to identify and treat any medical causes, and deal with any precipitants such as cessation of maintenance drugs, illicit drug use, and stressful life events. Prescribed antidepressants should be withdrawn as they may well exacerbate the elevated mood. Any treatments for past episodes should be reviewed and current long-term treatment optimised or restarted if stopped for any reason.

Depression

'I can honestly say that it's the most
torturous, relentless condition I've ever
experienced'

1. Can you describe a typical episode of depression?

Alastair: Depression, to me, is a mental and a physical thing.
It's so overwhelming you get no relief from it at all. You don't
even get comfort from sleep, but that's all you want to do.
Even putting a sock on is a chore, an effort. I can remember
staying with my parents and my mum saying, 'Alastair – clean
your teeth.' The very act of squeezing out the toothpaste
onto the brush – and I'm not exaggerating – was this huge,
almost unbearable effort. The simplest task becomes a major
chore, something you just don't want to do.

You don't want to speak to people either. If the phone
rang I wouldn't answer it. People would knock at the door
or ring the bell and I'd ignore it, hoping they'd go away. If
anyone came into the house I'd make sure I was in another
room, so I didn't even have to say hello.

Faye: I can so identify with that loss of motivation, the need to just hide away. Basically, you've had enough. You don't want to live anymore. You just want to make it all go away. I've made several attempts to kill myself – from the age of thirteen onwards. I think the last attempt I was about twenty-eight. I just couldn't see any way out of it. Nothing seemed to make it any better.

Now, where my moods are concerned, I'm extremely vigilant. I'm certainly more aware when I get depressed. Whenever my thoughts turn to self-harming I know how dangerous it is. I need to talk to a doctor, or my partner, as soon as possible.

For the last seven years I've been self-medicating with alcohol. I've used that instead of hurting myself physically, even though using alcohol is a form of self abuse, as I'm well aware.

Adam: The quick fix. Anything to get away from the pain you're going through.

Yes, it numbs all those feelings. The blackness, the loss of hope. In depression, these feelings are frightening, overwhelming. That's where I'm lucky having such an understanding partner. He doesn't really understand the depression, but he knows that for me it's really bad, and he will do absolutely everything in his power to help me get through it. He's cancelled work trips and appointments when he's felt that I needed him. Having his support is probably one of the biggest factors in stopping me going back into depression.

Adam: It's good to be in a relationship where the other person is supportive. But, unfortunately, not everyone is that understanding. Some people can't deal with the chaos it brings. With manic depression, relatives or partners have to cope with the two extremes. You've got the depression, where you're speechless, almost comatose in the corner, then the mania, where you're running round full of energy, bouncing off the walls, so to speak. It must be like living with two people. Your partner never quite knows who you're going to be from one day to the next.

Alastair: Depression is all-consuming. When it's at its worst you go beyond death. You go to that place where you think, all I want to do is die, because I know that if death means absolutely nothing at all, an eternal nothingness, then that is so much more preferable to the mood I'm in right now.

I like to play with my words, as you know. Mood spelled backwards is doom – and that's what it's like. One of my mantras during depression used to be, '*I want to die Today.*' I would repeat that over and over. Even watching the news could trigger the same yearning. I'd see a car crash, or a report that people had been killed in some accident and, without any form of self-pity, I'd think why wasn't *I* in that, why wasn't it me?

Faye: Did you ever try to take your own life?

Not consciously, no. Some people might say, well, if you felt so bad why didn't you commit suicide? But there's a very strong reason why I didn't. My friend's suicide in London affected me deeply. I realised how devastated the people around him were and how unable they were to come to terms with it. Those who love you the most are those that hurt the most. So I always felt that suicide was a big no-no.

Adam: For me, depression is almost beyond words. To someone who hasn't experienced the depths – what I would call clinical depression – it's hard to explain. There are varying degrees to the illness, of course. You could be suffering the milder form of depression, for instance, where you're still able to function to a degree. You carry on working, and just about manage to get through the day without being incapacitated in any significant way. Clinical depression is different. Clinical depression, I would say, is close to coma. Except, of course, in coma you can't feel anything at all.

One of the worst times for me was being told I was going to have ECT. My depression up until that point had been resistant to all other forms of treatment. So I signed the forms, or a member of my family signed them for me , and off I went to be wired up like Frankenstein's monster. The bizarre thing was, my initial reasoning for going along with it in the first place. I only agreed because the nurse assured me they gave you a general anaesthetic – and in my disturbed mind that was the most wonderful drug of all, even if it did only last a few seconds.

But, whatever the pros and cons of ECT, depression is so all-encompassing that you'd try absolutely anything to relieve it. I can honestly say that it's the most torturous, relentless condition I've ever experienced.

Faye: And you can't escape it. It's there as soon as you wake up in the morning.

Yes, in fact it's worse in the morning. I would wake early, usually around four or five, having spent most of the night staring into the darkness. Sleep, when it did come, gave no comfort at all – like blacking out and coming to again, with no relief the next morning. The concentration camp of the mind. You're a prisoner in your own head, being tortured on a daily basis. I don't use the analogy lightly either. Not having experienced physical torture, I wouldn't be able to compare the two objectively, but clinical depression is certainly unbearable in that you would do anything to escape it.

Alastair: It's that total deadness of everything, no positive feelings at all.

'I can so identify with that loss of motivation, the need to just hide away. Basically you've had enough. You don't want to live anymore.'

The reverse of the feelings you experience in mania, when all your senses are alive. The heightened awareness in depression is an awareness of self, of unendurable suffering replayed over and over. The only relief is medication, or whatever you can get from other sources. Alcohol sometimes works, but in this pitiful condition it often takes an extremely powerful sedative to have any affect at all.

Coming out of a depression, on the other hand, is incredible. I can't describe the relief. Like looking out over a tranquil bay with the sun coming up and clear blue skies all around. The nightmare, that has stretched on endlessly, consuming every waking moment, is finally over. You feel alive. You're in touch with everything around you, reunited with your family again. But in spite of any new-found optimism you might feel, you still have this dark memory buried deep in your psyche. An underlying fear of its return.

2. Were these episodes of depression shorter or longer than the episodes of mania?

Alastair: Longer, for me. A lot longer than the mania, which might last for a few days, sometimes weeks. With the medication I'm on now, Clopixol, I've learned to live with my illness. I've accepted it. But it does seem an endless slog at the time, having to battle through this utter deadness for so long. My depressions were probably eighty to ninety-percent compared to the manic phases. And it seemed to be either or – the mania or the depression – and nothing in-between.

Faye: Initially, the depression was longer. But as I've had the medication to balance it out, my moods are about the same at the moment. Obviously, I was depressed throughout all of my teenage years, then I had that huge high that lasted, on and off, for about a year. Since then the swings have been pretty equal.

I sometimes look back and try to work out what caused

that initial high. At the time, I'd left home and was living on my own. I'd also quit college and was doing my own thing, so this in itself gave me quite a lift. After that everything went skywards. My mood just went through the roof.

But the down times were so long and so bleak. Nothing ever changes in depression. You just know you're going to wake up and feel the same every day. It's that feeling of being pushed down people talk about. No matter what you do you can't seem to get out from under it.

Adam: The episodes of mania I had were catastrophic but much shorter. During the depressive periods my behaviour was fairly predictable. As you say, nothing ever changes. I didn't stay out all night causing trouble, or borrow huge sums of money to go off on wild sprees. That's why the partners of manic-depressives often say they prefer the spouse in the depressed state, purely because you don't pose the same threat to the marital home. You might be sat in a chair all day, staring at the walls, but at least you're not a danger in any way. You're just this morose shadow in the corner of the room, saying nothing, contributing nothing, locked in your own private world.

When I was manic, I was the opposite. An absolute nightmare to be around. A danger to myself and a burden to others. Psychotic and anti-social, completely out of control. People didn't know where I was going to turn up next, or even if I would still be alive. Depression is different, a kind of long endurance you have to cope with all on your own.

Alastair: Yes, the solitary aspect is the worst. Something far worse for you, the individual, than the mania, which tends to affect everyone else. With the mania, even though you can feel extreme anger and you're on fire, you're also alive in every sense. With depression, you're almost flatlining. It's just the nothingness. And the nothingness is darkness and hopelessness. It's like you're in the tunnel but there's no light at the end of it.

3. How does the possibility of a future bout affect your decision making?

Faye: It's a fear, definitely. Because I know that if I get really down again I'll end it myself. There's no two ways about it. I know exactly how I'm going to do it. Which method I'd use. It's set in my mind from past experience. Consequently I'm always checking on my mood thinking, how am I doing? What can I do to bring myself up? Am I slipping again? So, yes, it is a big fear for me.

Adam: When was the last time you suffered what you believe to be, a depression that bad?

Well, the last time I tried to kill myself I was twenty-eight. So that's ten years ago. Since then, I've dipped into depression quite severely a couple of times, but there have been mitigating factors. Recently I've had the support of my doctor and a counsellor I've been working with to help me get over it. So I've had the help I've needed. I've also managed to stay out of hospital, which is a really big thing for me. I absolutely hate being in hospital. All the people around me, the loss of control. I find the whole thing extremely traumatising. Six months ago they were threatening me with ECT again and I said: no way. I'll do anything but that. I don't want to go through that process again whatever happens.

Alastair: It's quite shocking to hear someone say outright that they would kill themselves, but that's the depths you can go to, isn't it.

It's the reality, unfortunately. You don't want to live like that anymore. You don't know how long it's going to last or if it's going to come back again. The only answer in the end is to look for ways to live with it, to balance it out in some way. It's learning, more than anything. Learning how to cope with it without being completely overwhelmed.

Alastair: Well, I don't suffer too badly from the depressive swings now, or at least, they're not as bad as they used to be. Once you've been to those levels, where you can't go any further down, you tend to be able to evaluate your moods with some clarity. As in mania, when you've been so high that you can't get any higher, you see your current moods in that light.

I tend to take things on a daily basis. I'm still on my medication. I've got a family, two young children. But it's difficult to plan things as such, because you don't know what state of mind you're going to be in in the future. Even going on holiday has a certain fear attached to it. Since being diagnosed bipolar I have had some pretty outrageous experiences abroad. The general excitement of being in a foreign country is often enough to spark a manic episode on its own. Then, back home, the elevated mood evaporates and depression kicks-in. It's like, 'Oh, God, I've met all these wonderful, exciting people and felt so fantastic, and now it's back to this boring, dreary old life again.'

Because of my illness, I don't believe that I could hold down a job. I seem to have at least one manic episode every year and it drains me completely.

Adam: Decision-making isn't so much of a problem for me these days. My illness doesn't stop me like it used to. But a lot of that is down to the fact that I no longer drink or take drugs. Even so, I always have to be aware of my capacity to go high and, conversely, to come down again. Manic depression has all these shades of mood right the way along the spectrum, with the extremes at either end. My intention is to try to stay somewhere around the middle, between these extremes, without going either way.

For years it was, literally, the rollercoaster for me. I was very rarely in the middle. Now, with a combination of medication, exercise and the abstinence I practise on a daily basis, I'm able to live somewhere in between.

I've often wondered if my depressive illness had anything to do with my drinking, which started around the same time. I'd begun to experiment with alcohol by then, but only on a recreational basis. I did get drunk one lunchtime and ended up attacking a boy in my class, but this was an isolated incident and certainly not typical of my normal behaviour. The connection between alcohol and depression is widely accepted, but in my case I'm not sure. Thousands of teenagers get drunk, without experiencing clinical depression as a direct result. My depression, I believe, pointed to some deep-rooted, chemical or biological problems that hadn't been treated.

But, in saying that, alcohol did go on to play a major role in the course of my illness, resulting in hospitalisation and preventing effective treatment for many years to come.

Chris's View

Many experiences recorded by service users can be seen as the early stages of a depressive phase. The most frequently reported early warning signs are loss of interest, an inability to put worries aside, interrupted sleep patterns, and feeling sad or tearful. The impact of such symptoms upon the individual can be considerable. Intervention by family members and care coordinators at an early stage can often reduce the risks of the relapse progressing and spilling over into other aspects of the patient's lives.

Below are some of the symptoms associated with the depressive phase:

- » Low in energy
- » Feeling tired/listless
- » Difficulty concentrating
- » Less talkative
- » Negative thoughts
- » Loss of interest in activities
- » Loss of interest in sex
- » Loss of appetite
- » Disturbed sleep pattern
- » Feeling anxious
- » Drinking alcohol too much
- » Using street drugs

As you can clearly see, all these symptoms might mean very little on their own. It is the presence of specific symptoms over a given period of time that can point to a potential relapse. Small changes in mood could be attributed to general tiredness or concern over a specific problem. But greater knowledge of EWS can lead to interventions designed to limit the effect of potentially serious changes. Making sure you sleep well, for instance – but at the same time limiting any urges to lie in bed for long periods. Making sure you have things to do – going out to meet friends and adhering to a routine. Trying to eat regularly and avoiding isolating yourself. Tracking these experiences and setting small goals, either on a day-to-day or weekly basis, can be extremely useful.

Early warning signs can be different for each individual, making identification and self-monitoring a key component in preventing relapse. Managing, or coping with depression involves a combination of anti-depressants and cognitive behavioural techniques (CBT). These techniques involve:

- » Thought monitoring
- » Mood diary
- » Thought channelling
- » Behavioural experiments
- » Developing Early Warning Signs Monitoring
- » Problem solving
- » Activity scheduling
- » Sticking with your medication

Developing a 'Time-Line' can be very effective. This traces life events along a chronological line, charting periods of change in mood, as well as the treatments and interventions that were useful. This will help identify potential patterns that emerge, and will demonstrate links between stress and the illness.

Depression, like mania, can lead to lengthy periods of unemployment and poor social functioning. It can also involve thoughts of suicide and feelings of hopelessness – a tremendously painful series of experiences that are often underrated by those close to the sufferer. The physiological presentation of depression, i.e. the absence of everything that contributes to make that person an individual, needs to be understood by the person themselves and those around them.

Developing insight is a key to managing bipolar disorder. Early intervention with triggers such as poor sleep or increased irritability can reduce the impact of depression. A greater understanding and ability to self-monitor is also essential in preventing relapse.

Treatment

'It's a kind of balancing act, I suppose. I don't always get it right'

1. Do you take medication to control your illness?

Faye: I'm on an awful lot of medication at the moment. I saw my doctor recently and he's trying to encourage me to bring some of it down. The problem with being at the limits with any medication is you've got nowhere to go if you get ill again. I'm currently on fluoxetine, metazepine, lithium and olanzapine. All really heavy doses, so I do need to start coming off them a bit, with the doctor's help.

The basic fear for me is that it will destabilise my mood. What effect will it have, coming off this high dose I've been on for so long? So it's trying to figure out the best and least traumatic way to do it.

Adam: That's the danger, isn't it, that you come to rely on medication too much?

Oh, it's a real fear, without a doubt. Then you come into the genetic side of it, the possibility that your brain chemistry is wrong. Do you, then, always have to take medication to counteract the affect of this? It's tricky. It's like an experiment you're conducting on yourself, where you sit back and await the results.

Alastair: When I was diagnosed with bipolar, the first thing they put me on was lithium. As I said before, lithium flattened me totally and turned me into a bit of a zombie. Basically, it took out my emotions and left me feeling lethargic and unresponsive. Nothing registered to me in that condition. Nothing at all.

Faye: How soon did you go onto lithium after you'd been diagnosed?

Almost straightaway. This was the early 90's – around 93, I think. And lithium really knocked me for six. I became totally emotionless, without any capacity for enjoyment whatsoever. After that I went onto a drug called carbamazepine, also known as Tegratol – a kind of lithium substitute. That seemed to work better with me, with far fewer side-effects. The purpose of lithium, as I understand, is to stop the highs and the lows. After all, that's what bipolar is. You have these huge, soaring highs and long, draining lows. Any drug you take, presumably, is to balance these devastating swings out. But I found (with lithium) that I just sank into depression. Carbamazepine seemed a little bit better. Not quite as severe.

I know that lithium works for some people, but it didn't for me. The side effects of carbamazepine were bearable, at least. With bipolar you tend to spend most of the time flat. It's just these brief periods of mania when you're on fire. Up there with the gods, so to speak.

Like Faye, I was also on olanzapine. This, as it was explained to me, was to stop me being delusional. When I'm manic, I get all these bizarre, obsessive thoughts.

I'm convinced I'm God. I'm convinced I'm the Devil. I'm convinced I'm the Messiah. The whole Allah business came about because of this strange preoccupation. I'd shorten Alastair to Allah, and refer to myself in this way, expecting other people to do the same. Olanzapine really does stop that obsessive thinking.

Adam: I was diagnosed around '92. Before then I'd just had these long depressive episodes that came and went of their own accord. In-between these, I suppose my moods fell in the normal range, although I tended to be on the withdrawn side. But in 1992 something major happened to me mentally. I just went through the roof. There didn't appear to be a catalyst for this, but it hit me hard. My first major manic episode tore through me like a hurricane.

Faye: Did you get the lithium treatment straight away?

Probably, although I can't honestly say without checking my medical records. I've been on so many antipsychotics over the years it's hard to remember. Like you, I was put on carbamazepine for a time. Then Largactil and Clopixol. But throughout most of the treatment I was drinking heavily, so the effects of any medication would have been cancelled out.

That's the trouble really. Because of the excessive drinking, I couldn't say whether the medication worked or not. Even without the drinking, I'm not sure I ever took it regularly enough. Then, as the years went on, I discovered drugs like diazepam and temazepam. This was the miracle cure I'd been looking for all along – a narcotic in pill form. I'd use them recreationally to get that special buzz. As I was always so full of tension and anxiety most of the time they were perfect. Mixing them with alcohol increased the effect tenfold. I abused these forms of medication for a number of years, specifically for that purpose.

There was a time, later on, when I was prescribed

diazepam by my doctor. My wife found an empty bottle one day and went ballistic, realising I'd been taking way over the prescribed dosage. She phoned the doctor, who immediately cancelled the prescription, and I was gutted. Absolutely gutted. I loved those things. They were a special lifeline to me that lifted my mood from the doldrums and helped me relax.

Alastair: I've also taken diazepam for years, which, incidentally, some people will know as Valium. I take that if I get a bit anxious. But I can often use it recreationally if I feel like getting a bit stoned. I'll up the dose. You know – take a handful of pills and get diazzied-out. Although this isn't an overdose in the conventional sense, I do take a lot more than the prescribed dose, which is why they're better off restricted.

I also take temazepam to sleep. Not every night, but most nights. Again, sometimes I'll use temazepam recreationally. Not to get to sleep, but just to get that feeling of being doped out and sedated. Sometimes I'd drink on it too.

But there is a downside, of course. You can build up a huge tolerance to these pills in a relatively short time, as you know.

Faye: What treatment would you like to have been offered?

I can't say exactly. Possibly more one-on-ones. Someone with a bit more understanding of the illness in general. The problem with medication – especially things like sleeping tablets, is they're so easy to abuse. You end up taking higher doses to try and level out your moods.

As for alternative forms of treatment, I really don't know. Maybe the cognitive therapies would help. They seem to work for some people.

Adam: Tablets are an addiction, like any other. I knew that

I could cash the repeat prescription from the doctor and, within minutes, I'd feel some relief. I used to call them 'floaters', because of that incredible feeling of buoyancy they gave you. I'd go from the doctor's to the chemist and straight round to my mum's, where I'd drop a couple of tablets immediately. The effects would kick-in about ten minutes later. But the next time I'd need three or four to get the same effect. That's how quickly you can build an immunity to the lower dose. As you say, the body can build up a huge tolerance for these things in a relatively short time.

Alastair: That's the other side to medication, isn't it. The recreational side. The deliberate abuse of prescription drugs to relieve the symptoms of mental illness. We've talked about things like lithium and carbamazepine, and olanzapine, which I tend to refer to as serious drugs. Whereas diazepam and temazepam are fun drugs. Just like cannabis or cocaine.

Faye: Until you develop a problem with them.

Oh absolutely! They're as dangerous as any street drug, perhaps worse. But from a personal point of view, they're the fun drugs. At least in my mind they are. You kind of look forward to them the way you would a holiday or a special treat. They're your friends. Much more like black market drugs but supplied legally.

2. Has hospitalisation been effective in stabilising your psychosis?

Faye: No. I have been admitted to hospital in the past, given ECT, and then been discharged with no follow up. While I was in there, I was given my medication and seen once in a while but there was no counselling, no therapy. I was just left to sit around the ward all day with all the other patients. Eventually, I thought, well, I'm going to have to convince them I'm well enough to go home. I can't take this anymore.

It's a big, big failing within the NHS. The fact that there is no therapeutic intervention other than the pills and the shock treatment they hand out. That's not to say that all the nursing staff are inept or uncaring, but there's a general level of apathy within the system because of the regime.

Adam: Staffing shortages and lack of resources.

Exactly. There was one nurse who organised Yoga sessions, and he was fantastic. But he was only part-time, once or twice a week. There was no structure to the day, apart from your meals and your medication. Nothing was actually done to help you get through such a traumatic experience. Nothing at all.

Alastair: My last manic episode was quite recent and extremely disruptive to both me *and* my family. Hospitalisation was effective in the end, but only because I was so desperate to get out of the place. I did what they wanted. It was a nightmare. As Faye says, you're shoved into a psychiatric unit with a lot of other people, all with different mental disorders, and left to get on with it.

When I first went into hospital I was completely manic. I'd be shouting and arguing with people. I'd get into fights with patients and insult members of staff. But, yes, it was effective ultimately because I would have done anything to get out. It's that feeling of being imprisoned, of being held against your will.

They changed my medication to a drug called Clopixol, in the form of a depot injection. This is a slow-release antipsychotic injection to stabilise your mood. They felt that the other stuff I'd been on – the carbamazepine and the olanzapine, wasn't particularly effective anymore. Normally I wouldn't have gone along with it. I'd been on carbamazepine and olanzapine for many, many years and been, sort of, stable. The thought of a change in medication was a big no-no for me. But, because I was so desperate to get out of there I agreed. I'd have taken arsenic if they'd have suggested it!

Now I take Clopixol, in the form of a depot injection once every fortnight. They gave me quite a high dosage initially to bring my mania down, which, as I said, was extremely high. I was in the psychiatric unit for about three months, which is the longest I've ever been hospitalised due to mania.

Faye: How did the hospital environment affect your mood?

It was awful. The patients on the ward are such a volatile lot. You don't know who you're dealing with. And, of course, while I was still high I was basically uncontrollable. They gave me the 200 milligrams of Clopixol every week to bring me down and, quite frankly, it turned me into a zombie. You develop this psychotic shuffle, where you just stumble along, with your shoulders hunched and your head down. You are – you're a zombie. That's the only word I can use to describe the way it hits you. It flattened me big time. So much so that I could hardly walk.

So yes, hospitalisation was effective in bringing my mania right down, but at a cost to my general wellbeing. I'm still on the same medication today, the depot Clopixol, but they've reduced it quite a bit. I'm taking a quarter of the amount now that I was when I was in hospital. Instead of 200 units a week, I'm getting 200 a month, which, I suppose, is an improvement.

Touch wood, the medication seems to be quite good. The thoughts of mania have totally dissipated. And I'm not too flat. I'd still say I'm depressed, but I'm not clinically depressed. I'm not suicidal. Everything's still a chore though. Absolutely everything. Washing. Eating. I get no real enjoyment from anything at all.

'I believe in medication and counselling. Talking about it, yes. That's what works, or has done for me before.'

Adam: My experience of hospitalisation is pretty grim, on balance. I don't have anything positive to say about any of my admissions to psychiatric hospitals. The only thing I will say, is that the extent of my mania was so severe on several occasions, that I needed to be taken off the streets for my own safety and, possibly, at times for the safety of other people. So in this respect, I believe hospitalisation serves a purpose, especially when someone is clearly psychotic and won't comply with treatment. What other option is there?

You reach a point during mania, when you lose all touch with reality. You're living in this delusional fantasy, where you're the number one player. With me, this became an absolute mission. I was about as far out on a limb as you can go, and I wouldn't be stopped by anyone.

Faye: Would you say you actually became a danger, then?

Well, yes, I would. But whether it was the fact I was in hospital, or the fact they were putting heavy dose of medication into me, I can't say. As soon as I came down I went into a sharp decline. From that elevated high of mania into clinical depression. So my memories of being in hospital are always tainted by this.

On the other hand, I can actually look back on the times I was psychotic with amazement. When you're manic, hospital is just one more place for you to act out your fantasies, your delusions. The staff, the patients – male and female, all seem to play along with this for a time, which can be hugely distracting. At one point I was having Chinese takeaways brought in, and guitars and amplifiers – in keeping with my rock star persona. One day, the Head Nurse came running into my dormitory room as I was playing an electric guitar, waving her arms around and shouting 'Adam – Please! Please! You've got to get all this out of here!' I thought it was the Hotel California and I was this, kind of, Jim Morrison character. The staff were all there to cater for me in every possible way.

Alastair: Absolutely! You get so delusional it's astonishing. Look at my behaviour when I'm manic. All that stuff about me being God and Allah and – more importantly – that everyone knows it. But people don't see you the same way you see yourself. They just think, 'Oh look, there's that mad bloke who thinks he's God. Let's keep out of his way.' Then you come across other manic depressives with all these different delusions. It's fascinating to see yourself in that context.

Adam: I remember coming to visit you in hospital. Your manic phase seemed to have lasted a long time, several weeks, which is surprising considering the medication they had you on. Then, weeks later, you began that slow decline into depression that's so indicative of the illness in general. Then you get the payback for that massive high, the flatness and the loss of energy.

Alastair: The two opposite poles again. Extreme happiness and utter depression. In mania, all your emotions are like touch paper. Then, when the touch paper's gone out, it's like you're dead. You have this body, but there's no soul there. No spirit. You're totally drained. Totally drained.

3. Have you been offered or considered any form of alternative treatment?

Faye: No. I'm a scientist. I don't believe in any of that alternative rubbish, I'm afraid. Sorry. I believe in medication and counselling. Talking about it, yes. That's what works, or has done for me before. Not someone trying to hypnotise you, or run their hands over your body to induce some sort of psychic change. The practical, proven approach is the only one I'd consider.

Adam: How about religion or any kind of faith to counter the downside?

Oh, I've had arguments about all that before. Long discussions with people about God. Frankly, I just don't see how you're supposed to put your faith in something you can't see, to get you through something as devastating as manic depression. I mean, personally, I don't believe in God, so where does that leave me?

I'm actually doing a lot of reading about Buddhism at the moment. I've got a book by the Dalai Lama in my bag. And I think, for me, that might be the way forward. I like the practical, down to earth approach, rather than the fantastical. The meditation aspect to still the mind.

Alastair: I believe that most treatment is pointless when you're seriously depressed. I really do. Careworkers and CPNs (Community Psychiatric Nurse) talk about the importance of doing things to keep active. Perhaps a college course, or some form of voluntary work. They talk about occupational therapy as if it's the answer to everything. When you're manic, you don't need motivation. You've got all the energy you could ever need! But coming out of that mania into depression, it's the complete opposite. You can't do anything. Even the thought of getting out of bed is too much to contemplate.

I tend to sleep a lot in this state. I don't read or watch TV. I don't ring my friends. Basically, I just stay indoors and hibernate. It's almost impossible to find motivation. You get offered all these things when you're flat, and you've come out of the mania. They say, 'Right – let's do this, let's do that.' And you're not physically able to do any of it. Nothing at all.

Adam: That was my experience after mania. That terrible feeling of lethargy, that I didn't want to do anything. But as far as any alternative treatment went, I don't remember being offered much at all. The only thing I did get, which everyone gets, was contact with a CPN, or a social worker, and I had several of those. One or two of them were actually very good. Others, I felt, could be patronising and didn't understand the problem at all. As you say, it's very easy to say to someone who's depressed, what you need is to go for a walk, or do a bit of gardening. But actually, the state of depression cuts you off from all that. You don't have the physical or mental capacity to think about it, let alone put it into practice.

You could argue that medication helped to bring me down from mania. But did it stabilise me? I don't know. I believe I'm more stable now, after years of fluctuating between the two extremes. But, as I've said before, a big part of my story is the fact that I stopped drinking, which had played a huge part in my illness right the way through.

The alternative treatments I've come across have really been the ones I've found myself, things I know help to keep me stable. Exercise, for instance. And sleep. I pay attention to these things because I know the triggers. I see myself as someone with a much more sensitive bio-system, if you like. Perhaps more sensitive than other people. So I have to be careful what I chose to do in case it leads me back down that same road. It's a kind of balancing act, I suppose. I don't always get it right.

Faye: Do you find it hard to remain stable?

Well, I tend to be drawn to extremes. Extreme exercise, for instance! Endurance events like the Ironman that take hours and hours to finish. Because I recognise this tendency in myself and relate it to my illness, I'm able to watch what I do, to think about the places my mind wants to take me.

But, it's interesting isn't it, the similarities in the illness, in the way it affects people, regardless of who you are. I mean, we're quite different in our upbringing and everything else, but we share so much in terms of the way the illness has affected us and changed our lives.

Alastair: The thing I find amazing about you, is that you've actually done it. You've gone out and done the exercise, the running and the cycling and all that. And Faye. Look how many marathons she's run, for Christ's sake! I think that's incredible.

I'm so often told by my Community Psychiatric Nurse that going for a walk is good for you. But how can you do that when you're the laziest person who ever lived! I am exceedingly idle, I admit that. How much of that is down to the depression I don't know.

Adam: The sense of apathy you feel is a well recognised part of the illness, isn't it. If you're slightly depressed you can respond to certain stimulus, or suggestions from people. You could probably even do certain activities at a push. But clinical depression is a different thing. People don't understand how it affects you.

Alastair: They have no idea. No idea at all.

Faye: It's the same with mania. People can be exuberant, can't they? Really outgoing, even a bit hypermanic. But the actual state of mania, as it relates to manic depression is a different thing. You can't say to someone who's manic, 'Now listen, you need to stop all that racing around and slow down a bit.' It simply wouldn't register.

But I also believe that you can't use it as an excuse. I don't want to be seen as a kind of victim without choices. I'm determined to live the life I want to live, and I'm prepared to fight for that, illness or no illness.

Chris's View

Treatment involves a combination of medication and psychosocial interventions (PSI). This can involve Cognitive Behavioural Therapy (CBT); this is not an 'alternative therapy', as described in some of the discussions, but is a recommended, evidence-based treatment.

Interventions will include medication and education, as well as advice about housing, support with employment, education targeted at the family, and one-to-one therapy.

Psychosocial Interventions (PSI) is a broad term used to describe a range of interventions that can be used to treat illnesses such as bipolar disorder. The overall aim of PSI is to reduce the stress of the experienced symptoms, improving the persons' capacity to cope, thereby promoting recovery.

Interventions include:

- » Standardised assessments
- » Psychological management of symptoms
- » Medication management
- » Relapse prevention
- » Family intervention
- » Psycho-education

All those who see specialist mental health services should receive a written care plan (known as CPA, or Care Plan Approach), receive a risk assessment, and details of how to access support in the event of a crisis or emergency.

The Care Programme Approach (CPA) was introduced in 1990 to provide a framework for effective mental health care for people with severe mental health problems.

Its main elements are:

» Assessing the health and social needs of those with specialist mental health needs
» Providing care needs, including housing, employment etc
» Working directly with those requiring more frequent and intensive medical intervention
» Working with those at risk of harming themselves or others

Interventions based on changing destructive thought patterns can have an equally beneficial effect. Cognitive Behavioural Therapy, as discussed in the last chapter, looks at challenging some of the beliefs held.

5 key areas have been identified as contributory factors in relapse:

» Environment
» Thoughts
» Emotions
» Physical feeling
» Actions

By looking at the way you view yourself and the world you live in, positive changes can be made. CBT focuses on improving how you manage the experiences of depression, anxiety or psychosis. Challenging thoughts and assumptions a person has can help reduce the impact of the illness itself.

Socratic Questioning can be an effective way of challenging unhelpful thoughts, by addressing negative assumptions a person has about themselves, in a gentle, non-confrontational way. Commonly heard thought patterns such as, *'Nothing ever goes right for me'* and *'Everyone hates me',* can, with help, be dispelled and more positive patterns introduced.

The initial focus is identification of the factors that act as a trigger to a given situation. An example might be a voice in your head telling you you're worthless. A secondary consideration is the understanding of how this is interpreted by the individual, and what feelings or thoughts occur as a result. Lastly, is the notion of response in the context of emotions, actions or physical feelings.

The ABC Model (Ellis, 1962) is an important concept of CBT. Through the use of Socratic questioning, this model can be used in clarifying the link between emotional distress and psychotic symptoms experienced. This approach is based on the assumption that a person's response to a problem is central to the nature and context of how it is experienced.

The Family

'My illness had a terrible effect on my ability
to be a parent'

1. How has your illness affected your family?

Alastair: Well, it's affected my family in a devastating way. My father was very successful. He ran the medical branch in the Air-Force, and he also got a Knighthood from the Queen. I'm the only son. Of my two sisters, one's just qualified with a Law degree, in her early-fifties – she's also been successful as an estate agent and a property developer etc. My other sister's the Co-President of an international record company, so she's been very successful, too. Whereas me? I'm just the waster of the family. I've taken drugs. I don't work. I've achieved nothing. I know that all sounds terribly dramatic, but that's how it is.

Faye: Is that how your family see you, or is that how you see yourself?

Perhaps a little of both, I don't know. But I do know the

trouble I've caused them when I've been manic. I put them all into a vortex every time I get sectioned, especially when the mania is at its height. I become rude and abusive, sometimes even threatening. It's a nightmare. Then my parents have to come and visit me in hospital, and it's a real drag for them, too.

I can remember being on the phone to my mother, all bitter and twisted, saying things like, 'Lady Donald, if you don't come and get me out of here, I'm going to commit suicide, and it'll be all your f---- fault!' When you're delusional, you don't care. You're very selfish. And, of course, my family worry about me because blood's thicker than water.

So, yes, I've put my family through huge amounts of stress. They don't like coming to visit me in a psychiatric unit because it's not a nice place to be. I sometimes feel that I'm a huge disappointment to them, perhaps because they don't understand bipolar. They don't understand that it's an illness like any other, that I can't really help it.

Faye: It's been very tough for my family. Mum has got absolutely no understanding of mental illness. Her attitude is, 'Pull yourself together and get on with it.' My dad reacted very badly and I suffered for that. Between the age of eighteen and twenty-two, at the height of my depression, we didn't speak. And even after that, when I was in hospital, he would drive Mum over to visit and sit in the car while she came in. He wouldn't come in to see me himself because he just couldn't cope with it. He understood, though. He knew what I was going through, but he still couldn't bring himself to reach out and offer that extra bit of support that I needed so badly.

It's getting better, I have to say. I've told them both I've been working on this book, and Mum said, 'Oh, I'll be interested to read that.'

Alastair: Really? My goodness!

Yes, that's what I thought. My God, Mum, do you know what you're letting yourself in for! But Dad said it sounded like a really worthwhile project. I think they're more open now than they were in the past. They've got a bit older and, perhaps, more understanding. I'm also older, of course, with more understanding and experience of coping with the illness. When I was a teenager it was a nightmare. It was a war zone. It really was.

Adam: It's so difficult, isn't it, especially when you feel members of your family don't understand. I can remember walking along the beach with my dad one day. I was really depressed, and he wanted to try to help me. So we're walking on this lonely strip of sand, with the waves breaking on the shore – I'm utterly down and barely able to speak. And he looks at me and says, 'I didn't know you got depressed.' I was absolutely astounded by that. In all the years of me being crippled by this illness, he had no idea.

Faye: He didn't know you that well, after all.

When you're depressed, I suppose you can blank everything off. People might not necessarily know you were feeling that way, they might just think you were in a bad mood or whatever. One of the frustrations of depression is the inability to convey the depth of what you're going through to other people. It's the silent scream. The awful isolation of being trapped in a dark room with no one to listen.

Faye: Yes, that's definitely the worst aspect of depression, apart from the pain itself. That feeling of being cut-off from everyone and everything, especially your own family who know you better than anyone else.

I really felt that separation with Dad when he wouldn't

visit me in hospital, although I understand his reasons better now. I think, generally, people don't know how to deal with you. Unless they're trained in dealing with people with mental health issues, they just don't know what to do.

Alastair: Separation is awful. I've got two kids and I adore them. Prior to me being sectioned this last time, I hadn't been sectioned for at least ten years. I remember thinking, this will never happen to me again. I will never allow myself to get so bad. How wrong I was. 2012 was a dreadful year for me. People were predicting the end of the world, the end of the Mayan Calendar and all that business. Well it felt like the end of the world for me, too. I got sectioned in April, 2012. To me, April is an anagram/acronym for Al Rest In Peace. So I kind of thought, right, I'm dying this year, I have to do something to save the world! My delusional thinking ran to its usual extremes but on an even more drastic level. You know. No one else can do it because I'm the Chosen One. The Messiah. Even though, the other half of me thinks I'm the Devil.

Faye: Then, once the illness reaches that stage, you're not listening to anyone.

I couldn't agree with you more, Faye. In that regard, it is totally selfish. As I said, I've got two kids, and I'd never been sectioned as a father before. This was the first time that's happened. One of the aspects of mania is the irrational anger you feel, and this can be directed at anyone, even the people who care about you. I would sometimes ring the house and leave a message for the kids, saying I hoped they were well and having a lovely day at school etc, etc. Then I'd leave a horrible message for my long-suffering partner of about seventeen years, saying how much I despised her and how I wanted her out of *my* house. Obviously, these things are said in the height of mania and don't have any rational basis at all. But they are extremely hurtful to the people who care about you, who've done nothing whatsoever to deserve them.

2. How do you think family members view the disruption to home life?

Adam: I'd never really stopped to think how my illness had affected my family until some years later. Then I realised the damage I'd done. Manic depression is such a devastating illness. Unless you're on the outside looking in, it's hard to assess the real damage. But I have some idea, through speaking to members of my family, as to what it was like. That's one of the aspects of the illness that's so hard to confront. The devastation it causes families. Not only the sufferer, but everyone else involved as well. What I put my wife through and, obviously, my son when he was very young.

When I was manic, I'd often just leave the house at all times of the day and night. I'd be watching television, or listening to music on headphones, then suddenly I'd be gone, out the door. I'd walk for miles, often all night. I wore down pairs of shoes with all the walking I did. I'd be exhausted, shattered, but somehow I'd keep going, only to burn out spectacularly at some later date.

When I think of how I was then, I can't help thinking of that cartoon character. The whirling dervish. What was his name?

Alastair: Tasmanian Devil?

Adam: That's it. The Tasmanian Devil. It must have been like having one of those in the house, spinning out of control. It certainly was for *my* family. But as I said, it wasn't until much later that I found out exactly how my erratic behaviour had affected them.

Faye: My illness hasn't really affected my family to that extent, because the mania didn't start until after I'd left home. But it has affected relationships with previous partners – especially with my husband when I was going in and out of hospital and he couldn't cope with it. He had no understanding whatsoever of what I was going through. He was in the Navy, so he'd be away for six months at a time.

Alastair: How long were you married?

For about six years. But, as I said, he was away a lot during that. Most of my down times happened while he was away, so he never saw how bad I was getting.

I've been really lucky with my current partner, in that he's been prepared to listen and understand. And that, I think, is the hardest thing of all. Getting people to understand the illness from your point of view. How you think and how you feel, and how it affects your ability to communicate when you're going through a rough time. Having someone who's caring and considerate can make all the difference. Not everyone has that.

Alastair: And not everyone can cope with the extremes of the illness, can they. It's too much to expect a spouse or a partner to put up with it for any length of time. It's not just mental, it's physical too. These enormous surges of energy you feel. Incredible bursts of fearlessness and power that take you over.

I totally understand how you can be listening to music one minute then gone the next! Off on some mad adventure, inspired by the thoughts in your head. When I'm manic, music overwhelms me. I become obsessed with it, completely transfixed.

But regarding my family, I feel as guilty as hell. Dreadful. If it wasn't for my partner I'd be dead. Or, I'd be in prison or a psychiatric unit. Because I can't look after myself. I have trouble motivating myself. Even getting out of bed is a huge chore, so I tend to lie there sleeping, not wanting to face the world.

3. Do you think your illness affected your ability to be a parent?

Faye: Well, as I don't have children, I suppose this question doesn't apply directly. But the illness has certainly influenced my attitude towards having children, and made me think a great deal about the ramifications. When I was married, we were trying for a baby and I was aware, at the time, of the medication I was taking and the risk of post-natal depression. But we decided to go for it anyway and, fortunately, nothing happened. Eventually we split up.

Since then, the severity of my illness and the medication I've been on, has coloured any decision as to whether I have children or not. My dad's depression, compared to mine, was quite mild. Mine was quite extreme. So how extreme might it be for any child of mine? I know that science and medication are advancing all the time, but you can't say with any certainty that you could predict the way it's going to be in the future. Not where your children are concerned, anyway.

I'm not going to have kids now. That's not an option. But it was a source of anxiety for a long time, weighing up all the different possibilities in my head.

Alastair: On the question of parenting, I have to say yes. Big time. The illness has totally affected my ability to be a parent. My partner does everything. If I can get away with doing absolutely nothing, that's what I'll do. That's the option I will go for every single time. But she's quite a strong woman. She makes me do things, in the end, to stop me from wasting away completely. If I didn't have her, I don't know what I'd do. I'd have no one – not even myself. Left to my own devices, I would do nothing. I'd live on cereal. I'd never wash. I'd never get out of bed.

'I'd never really stopped to think how my illness had affected my family until some years later. Then I realised the damage I'd done.'

Faye: Have you always been like this – reliant on other people?

Not always no. There was a time when I was quite independent, when I was younger certainly. But over the years, the illness takes its toll. You don't have the ability to bounce back so easily. I need someone there to look after me. Because, when I'm flat, the low self-esteem is overwhelming. That feeling of, 'Oh, God, I am totally useless.'

The only benefit of being bipolar, when you're in the depressed state, is that you have no fear of death. That's an appalling thing to say, I know, because I'm a parent with two kids. But the thought of dying when you're in that state is actually quite comforting.

Adam: That's something we haven't touched on in any depth so far – suicide. But, definitely, my illness had a terrible effect on my ability to be a parent. I know it did. Certainly my ability to bring up my son – although he tells me now that there were good times as well. And, yes, there were good times. Taking him to football, for instance. I'd regularly attend his training sessions and matches, and support him whenever I could. But the drinking, the depressive phases, the mania and the hospitalisations, all these would have an inevitable cumulative effect. The illness itself tears the whole structure of family life apart in the end.

So it's with some sadness that I look back on those days. I remember one particular time, when I was in a psychiatric hospital, and I can remember this clearly. My wife brought my son up to visit, when he was about six, or seven. I was in a complete clinical depression then. Pretty much comatose. We walked from reception round to the back of the hospital. It was a lovely, sunny day with quite a few people sat around. They even had two mini goalposts set up on the grass. My son started kicking a football around, quite happily, while we were sat on a bench watching. I felt completely isolated and cut-off from everyone. I was this lifeless shell, unable to speak. And that cuts you deep inside. Something as powerful and destructive as that you don't forget. To be emotionally dead like that, without even the ability to reach out to your own son. That's a horrible experience to have.

Thankfully, today it isn't like that. I have a great relationship, not only with my son, but with all the members of my family. Being relatively stable over the last few years has allowed me a sense of freedom from the restrictive nature of the illness. I know it'll always be with me in one form or another but I'm no longer ruled by it completely.

Faye: There was an awful lot of guilt around my dad and his illness. The fact that I was now ill as well. He did blame himself, I know, even though it wasn't his fault. I mean no parent would ever wish to induce something as devastating as bipolar in any of their children, would they. It just causes so much confusion and frustration. You want to explain to them how you're feeling but you can't, you're locked in behind this wall of silence, and it's really difficult to breakout.

Adam: It's poignant in many ways, isn't it? Depression is worse because it's a pain no one can see. I can remember my mum taking me to see a psychiatrist once, years ago when I was about fifteen. Having suffered badly with depression since my teens, I know what it feels like. The difference between clinical depression and just feeling a bit down. So I sat next to my mum, and the psychiatrist was sat behind his desk looking at me. And my mum said, 'I've brought Adam along because he's very depressed.' He looked at me for a moment and said, 'Well, you don't *look* depressed.' I couldn't believe it. Hearing him say that was another form of torture. I just sat there thinking, if you could spend ten-seconds inside my head.

Faye: You'd know what it was like.

Adam: You'd know exactly what it was like – and you wouldn't need to keep making such inane comments!

Alastair: That's the trouble, isn't it. People who don't have bipolar, or haven't suffered clinical depression, don't really know what it's like. Even doctors and psychiatrists don't really know. You hit the highs and everything's full-on a hundred-percent. Then comes the awful flatness when everything dies and you can't get out of the chair. These experiences drain you completely.

And the family suffer the most. Particularly in depression. Your child just becomes a thing. I know that's an awful thing to say, but it's true. It's not even *your* child. It's not even a human being. It's a thing running up and down getting in your space. You feel no emotion towards it whatsoever.

Adam: You know on an intellectual level that you have love for your child, but depression cuts you off from that feeling.

Alastair: Totally.

Faye: I don't have children, but I know that feeling so well. You're unable to respond to anything or anyone. That's the despairing nature of the illness. And from other accounts of depression I've read, that's what it's like for most sufferers. It's that deadening of the spirit. At least with most other emotions you can feel – things like sadness, anger, and rage. You're in touch with them. You're alive. Depression cuts you off from all that. I think depression must be the closest thing to death you can experience while still being alive.

Alastair: Oh, it is. Death is Nirvana when you're depressed. That's the truth.

But I have to say that it was my family that stopped me attempting suicide. I've seen the pain and anguish it causes when someone takes their own life. The thought of my children growing up without me was too much to bear. But, in saying that, I can understand what makes people do it, I really can.

Adam: That's the paradox, isn't it. The only solution you can see to the pain you're going through is to end it permanently, causing even more pain and suffering to the ones you leave behind.

Chris's View

The conflicting symptoms of bipolar disorder make a severe impact on both social and personal relationships. Unfortunately, there isn't one specific guidebook that will answer all the questions a family member might have, or map out exactly what to do to manage a particular situation. By maintaining an honest, open approach, damage to relationships can often be repaired and a stronger, healthier environment created for all concerned.

Families can often feel totally overwhelmed watching the person they love become unwell. Below are some of the challenges attributed to bipolar disorder.

- » Disruption of family routine
- » Financial strain
- » Grief
- » Social isolation
- » Marital problems
- » Challenge to parenting skills
- » Feeling trapped
- » Crisis of depressive/manic episode
- » Stigma
- » Lack of Information
- » Access to services
- » Resentment
- » Guilt

As well as the shock and confusion that can arise, there can also be anger, loneliness and denial. Help for the family can mean intervention from the services who then offer a range of support components.

These may include:

» Engagement of family
» Education
» Communication training
» Goal setting
» Problem solving
» Self-management
» Increasing family wellbeing
» Maintenance of skills

The family is an important part of any individual's environment and, therefore, holds great importance when considering mental health. A caregiver is anyone close to the sufferer who supports and helps them manage the illness within their personal life. One study, Priebe et al (1989), shows that patients with bipolar disorder show significantly poorer treatment responses when faced with critical comments and over-emotional involvement from relatives.

One way some family members have of coping, is to draw a clear distinction between the person they love and the detrimental effects of the illness. In doing so, they are recognising that their relative bears no responsibility for the onset of the condition and, therefore, cannot be blamed for its consequences.

Within a marriage, the effects of mental illness can be destructive, adding pressures which can be hard to withstand. However, while having a spouse who is suffering from a mental illness can cause extra strain, being married can also be an advantage to a person with bipolar disorder. In a Finnish study of young adults with mental illness, positive changes in symptoms and social activities were most common among those who were living with a spouse (Wade and Pevalin 2004).

The Wellness Recovery Action Plan, or WRAP (Copeland 1997) is a programme planned by the clients, with support by those around them. The client builds a toolbox which includes a daily plan, early warning signs, trigger plan and a crisis plan, which they and their families can use to stay well. WRAP helps people get back on the road to recovery after a crisis, teaching them crucial problem solving skills and how to keep a healthy mind and body.

The Social Impact

'The wider context is the cost to all the
services who have to come in and bail you
out'

1. How do you see the cost of your illness in a wider context?

Alastair: Well, in financial terms it's been considerable:
I get money off my parents, to support me, on top of the
support I've had from the state when I've been ill. Doctors,
psychiatrists and hospitalisations. All of that adds up in the
end. So, in that respect, I've cost quite a lot. Do I have guilt
about it? Yes, I do. Mainly because I had a public school
education and I thought I'd be successful and life would
be a blast. Things would be easy and I'd sail through. But
that hasn't been the case. At times I've struggled to cope.
That's not an easy thing to admit, but it's true.

    With my friends it's been a similar story. I can remember
my partner ringing one of my friends after I'd been out for
a long weekend when I was living in London. She wanted
to know where I was, as I'd gone out with hardly any money.
My friend laughed and said, 'Listen – you'll be surprised
how long Alastair can make a tenner last!' Even my friends

paid for me because they knew I wasn't working. They knew that I was skint, so they'd buy me drinks and entertain me all night. I had a good friend who kept me supplied with drugs. He'd give me cocaine and pay for me to get into clubs. This was nothing unusual. It happened all the time.

Adam: But you weren't always like that, surely?

No, I wasn't. When I was younger I worked hard and paid my way. But as time went on and my mental state worsened, I found it increasingly harder to fit back in. This is the first period of stability I've had for years, and that's no exaggeration.

Faye: I see myself as very separate from the world. I have family but I don't have friends. I don't work either – at the moment. So yes, I would say, my illness has negatively influenced my ability to hold down a job and be a 'normal' member of society, whatever that is. There's been a huge cost to the state in terms of medication and hospital fees.

But I have always maintained the desire to one day take my place and be a self-supporting member of the community again. That is my ultimate aim.

Adam: Not to be held back by your illness in any way.

Yes, I really believe so. It's so easy to fall into the trap of thinking you can't do anything else, that the cushion the state provides prevents you from being independent. But, ultimately, I've got too much pride. I want to do something. I want to be somebody. I want to be able to say to my dad, 'Look, you can be proud of me.' I think it all comes down to this in the end. To break out of the role of victim and be someone else, someone you can be proud of.

My long-term aim is to go to Open University and get my degree, then go into teaching. That, to me, would be the ideal scenario, something I've wanted to do for a long, long time.

Adam: The cost has been huge for me, too, especially regarding my ability to work and to function in society. I was self-employed continuously from the age of sixteen, right up to the point when my marriage broke down and I became unable to work any longer. My illness got steadily worse. The drinking, the depression, the mania. Everything seemed to get worse. And – I think that word you used is so apt to describe the condition – I just became a victim. Like Alastair, I too had some really good friends who would take pity on me and buy me drinks in the pub. It almost became the done thing. You know. 'Poor Adam. He's just come out of the nuthouse, he can't pay.' That happened again and again, throughout the years that I was unemployed, going in and out of hospital. At the time I wasn't aware of the implications. It was only looking back on it years later that I realised how much I'd fallen into that way of behaving.

And you're right. It is difficult to climb out of the trap. When you've lived that rollercoaster – all the highs and the lows – and you've got the support system of the state, your friends and family and everyone else involved, it can be very difficult to step outside of that. The fear is always that you're going to be plunged back into a bout of depression, or mania, and not be able to support yourself. It isn't easy to break out of that way of thinking. But I know it can be done. Like you, my pride won't let me be perceived as a victim.

Alastair: Yes, it is a trap. You feel completely and utterly trapped. And also, I would say, when you're manic, money means nothing. It's like, if you've got the money you can squander it. Money has no real value, as such.

Adam: It's like you own the Bank of England.

'Most of the people who know me would say I'm outgoing and gregarious most of the time, Being bipolar has just led me to the extremes.'

Alastair: Absolutely. Money is nothing. You want to say to everyone, 'Look, I am priceless. So if you've got a bit of filthy old dosh, spend it on me!'

But again, it's that delusional thinking that causes so much trouble. You go from that total, chaotic irresponsibility that's the hallmark of mania, to that awful realisation that comes over you in depression. Then you can evaluate the cost in wider terms, as you say. Only then does it become more apparent.

Faye: And it's the cost to your own family. Like a microcosm. The wider context is the cost to all the services that have to come in and bail you out. The state, the hospitals, the police stations. All these things. Then there's the endless round of doctors, psychiatrists, and healthcare professionals you have to see in order to treat your illness. The list goes on ad infinitum. And, when you're manic, you don't care about any of it.

Adam: It's never just one person suffering from an illness in isolation, is it. It's always the wider impact. The spider web, with you, the supposed victim, trapped in the middle. The manic episodes are like a rebellion against all that. A kind of emotional and mental breaking-out of the straightjacket of depression that's held you down for so long.

2. Can you put the stigma of mental illness in a social context?

Alastair: Not so much when I'm manic, as I don't have the awareness. But certainly when I'm either level, or depressed. I just feel like a lesser human being. I can't function normally. I'm basically a drain on society. And because of this I have very low self-esteem. It's just this feeling of uselessness, that I'm a bit of a leech, a bit of a parasite.

I also believe there are too many people on the planet. And I can't help feeling that I'm the lowest of the low, sometimes. Maybe I shouldn't be here at all. What's the point in me being here? I'm a drain on society and that kind of thing. Now I'm starting to sound a bit like Hannibal Lecter, aren't I!

But seriously. I'm sure you get the gist of what I'm saying. And remember, these are the low points we're talking about here. Most of the people who know me would say I'm outgoing and gregarious most of the time. Being bipolar has just led me to the extremes.

Faye: Because I don't have that many friends, and I've been quite isolated within society, there aren't that many people who know about my illness. When I am in contact with people, for whatever reason, I'm able to be quite open with them. I don't feel the need to hide behind my illness. If I trust someone I can say to them, 'Look, this is the way I am.' And so far people have been pretty understanding.

The last time I had someone to confide in was in hospital. She was having treatment for depression and we became quite close. But generally I avoid situations where I feel obligated to explain. I find it's better to keep myself to myself in the long run. Mental illness is still a subject most people find hard to understand.

When I first met my partner I had this huge inner struggle as to when, or even *if*, I should tell him. I'd been seeing him for about a week, socially, and we'd been out a few times. In the end, I wrote him this huge, long letter explaining how I was. Basically, giving him the choice. You know, saying, 'This is how I am, it's up to you whether or not you think you can cope with it.'

Alastair: That's one way of handling it, I suppose.

Well, yes. But I felt so anxious about it, that it was such a big thing. I suppose I wanted to give him the opportunity to back out if he felt he wasn't up to it. And, thankfully, he understood. He was really supportive.

Adam: I felt the stigma right from my first hospital admission. I'd always feared, right from an early age, that I would end up there, or in a similar institution. Something in the back of my mind – a premonition, I don't know. Then, lo and behold one day, there I was. It seemed like a self-fulfilling prophecy playing itself out. I thought, this is it. I'm fated to be this way for the rest of my life.

As soon as I came out of hospital I was plunged back into my normal life. Friends, family, work, and everything else. Everything went on the same as it did before, with only one difference. I now had a major mental illness – officially!

Although I remember my friends being very good, there was still that element of misunderstanding. Not knowing what everyone else was thinking or saying behind my back. Occasionally there'd be a bit of a joke, 'Lookout – what's Adam's going to do next?' That kind of thing.

Faye: Whispers in the background.

Inevitable, really. You're always aware of it at the back of your mind. Whenever I went into a pub, or wherever I happened to be working, it was the same feeling. You're always aware of the impression you might be making on people you've never met before, who may have heard stories about you. Maybe they weren't thinking these things at all, but it didn't matter. It's a difficult thing to deal with.

I came across a word in a book I was reading that leapt out at me. Unworthiness. Not worthlessness, or lack of worth, but *un-worth-iness*. And I think that can happen if you're not careful. The stigma of having a mental illness can have that effect on your outlook. Initially, it takes a lot of conscious effort to overcome these difficulties. Once you've had a mental illness, there is always going to be a certain stigma to it, mainly from people who don't understand. But it's down to you in the end, as to how you deal with it. You can't afford to let it bring you down.

But look at the statistics. We're all susceptible in varying degrees. That's what people fail to recognise. Everyone on this planet is capable of becoming mentally ill at some point. Through conflict, illness, bereavement, and a whole range of different circumstances. That may not be a comfortable fact to deal with but it's true.

Alastair: Of course it is. And it's not something to be ashamed of, either, even though it makes you feel that way at times. It's almost as if you have to explain yourself in social situations. You find yourself saying your name, and in the next breath adding, 'Oh, and I'm also bipolar.' like a, sort of, qualification.

Some of my friends used to introduce me to their friends as, 'Mad Al', and, sometimes I would get a bit aggravated by this. Why couldn't I be, 'Normal Al', instead of, *'Mad* Al'! Immediately you've been given the persona of a lunatic, whether you like it or not.

Faye: People can be really insensitive, even when they think they're being funny.

Adam: I was once introduced to a group of people by a friend of mine as ' *The lunatic.'* Now, I had a split-second decision whether to flip my lid at that point, and go ballistic, or just laugh it off. So I laughed it off. But I remember going to see my dad, absolutely furious, and telling him. My dad shook his head and said, sort of, philosophically, 'Well, what can you do? I'm sure it was just a joke. He didn't mean anything by it.'

Obviously, there were times when I *was* a lunatic. Certainly, my behaviour during mania wasn't that of a sane person. But it doesn't make it any easier to hear it said like that in front of people.

Alastair: No, it doesn't. Because you're not insane, you just have an illness. But, at the end of the day it's a, sort of, paradox, isn't it. After all, when you're in that manic state, you *are* a lunatic! At least, with bipolar you are. There's no other word for it.

Adam: Yes, you are. You're absolutely beyond any help at that particular time. One of the problems these days is the way the whole thing's perceived in the media. They say the stigma's not so bad now, as people are much better informed about the illness, which is probably true. In the past there have been famous writers and artists who've been manic depressive, but it wasn't so well known. Now we have celebrities regularly appearing in the news. But for these people it's different. It's seen as just another aspect of their famous personality, a kind of intriguing quirk, so to speak. When you're Joe Bloggs, living on a council estate, you're just another statistic. You're not accorded the same status.

Alastair: Absolutely. You don't have that same prestige as famous people. I think it's important to make that distinction.

3. Has increased public awareness made any difference to the problem overall?

Alastair: Not to me really. Not that I know about it anyway. But then I don't read all that much. I don't watch TV. So I don't really know. But this runs on from the last point we were talking about. That it's almost become a bit fashionable to say you're bipolar. I've heard that before. People suddenly announce 'Oh, I'm bipolar.' Because they think it gives you an excuse for random behaviour.

Adam: They think it's cool in some way.

Alastair: Yeah. To be a bit off the wall. You're not normal, you're quirky. And if you can come up with something outrageous, it's even better, 'Oh, I'm sorry, but I'm bipolar.' That sort of thing. It can be seen as an excuse.

Faye: I don't believe that the public really are all that aware. I think there's still a lot of confusion around the issue. I've definitely shied away from dealing with other people over the years, mainly because I don't know how they'll cope with my fluctuating moods. Generally, it's frustrating to have to think like this, especially when you've got hopes and dreams. I want to get into mainstream life, work, and study etc, but as I don't know how I'll be from one day to the next, I find it difficult. I'm always wary of exposing myself to the outside world.

Adam: Yes, it's easy to feel isolated by other people's perceptions, whether they're accurate or not. Mania and depression are extremes on a spectrum, aren't they? Ordinary human behaviour can be found all the way along that spectrum, without the need to be treated by drugs. Most people manage to balance out their mood swings between these extremes. Manic depressives aren't always that successful.

But I think Alastair's right. There has been a tendency in the last decade or so for the illness to become a bit, fashionable.

Alastair: I'm a bit off the wall because I'm bipolar.

Adam: Exactly. But there's nothing remotely fashionable about being in a psychiatric hospital having ECT. Or being physically manhandled down to the lock-up unit by six members of staff because you threatened one of them with a pool cue. That's the reality for some of us. That's the illness at the extreme end.

Faye: I suppose that's where the media play a part in educating the public, who have no idea what it's really like. But I'm still not convinced that this leads to more sympathy and understanding. People generally shy away from subjects like mental illness, because they're fearful. It's like being confronted with some aspect of yourself you can't deal with. As you said before, anyone can become mentally ill through a variety of different reasons. But, in saying that, I do believe that some of us are born with the illness. Or, at least, the genetic traits that make development of the illness possible.

Alastair: Absolutely.

That's why it's important not to feel marginalised and left out. Having an understanding partner is important, as I said earlier, but you can still feel isolated no matter what your situation. Society's way of dealing with the problem is to ignore it, basically, and pretend it doesn't exist. I don't mean that in terms of the services and organisations set up to help, and all the dedicated individuals within that framework, but in terms of the public's attitude. They don't know how to deal with it, so they'd rather ignore it and hope it goes away.

Chris's View

Effective intervention by care coordinators can lessen the burden on the state and ease the suffering of both client and family. The aims of any such interventions are to:

- » Promote hope
- » Independence
- » Increase coping
- » Recovery
- » Improved long-term prognosis

People with severe bipolar disorder often have smaller social networks than others and tend to be in more dependant relationships. Simply being with someone during a period of severe mental illness can be difficult, often requiring hospitalisation and involvement of social services.

Good social support can provide help in a variety of ways, including:

- » Information
- » Integration into a social group
- » Act as a 'buffer' to stress

Vital to the process, is a 'therapeutic alliance' between the practitioner and client; this might mean the Mental Health Team, or a single professional who engages with the service user. The working relationship that arises from this is based upon trust and honesty, and is effective at supporting the individual. Indeed, successful collaborations are seen to be pivotal in developing a sense of hope in each client, giving them the necessary foundation from which to continue.

Practicalities aside, there are also the emotional, psychological and physical effects of caring for someone, whether elevated in their mood or depressed. Having people close to you who are equipped with knowledge and can help is essential.

Think about:

» Sharing your Early Warning Signs
» Sharing your service contact details so others know who to contact
» Sharing your CPA documentation
» Keeping a log on your contacts with services and what you are told
» Learning what your illness means
» Learning and teaching others about your medication
» Having a 'Crisis Plan'. Who will you or others contact?

This could mean allowing certain people to check in with you to see how you are, or being accompanied to appointments with the mental health team; accepting advice from those close to you about your health, taking regular exercise, and realising that it's no one's fault you have this illness

So what is recovery exactly? It is more than a collection of ideals, concepts and self-evaluations. It is *how you live,* not just whether you are well or unwell, or whether or not you've been in hospital. It is *a journey* that can be measured and talked about, pinpointing ways a person can engage in wider society.

Recovery can involve:

» Reintegration into normal activities that were temporarily stopped
» A new freedom to practice rights and not feel excluded
» Knowing you are much more than a diagnosis
» Re-connecting with education and leisure activities

» Regaining confidence, self-esteem, and physical fitness
» Enjoying stability in mood
» Contacting friends and regaining independence
» Equality in wider society
» Ability to succeed, to feel happy and fulfilled, and to make the most of life in spite of illness

It can be helpful to see recovery as taking control, and yourself as the 'director'. By pacing yourself and setting personal boundaries you begin to change and grow. With help, it is possible to make a full recovery.

» Use control as a strength in recovery
» Practise self-acceptance
» Explore the role of spirituality
» Understand that while medication helps you manage your illness, *you* manage your life

Knowing yourself is the cornerstone of recovery. Look to enhance the following four concepts:

» Self-confidence
» Self-esteem
» Self-awareness
» Self-acceptance

Learning to cope with the illness might mean being more creative, and continuing the development of one's personality. Instead of feeling guilty, allow yourself to feel 'bad' if that is how you feel. Reflect on your inner experiences and build hope and optimism.

Coping Strategies

'I have hopes and dreams like everyone else
and I want to fulfil them'

*1. How does manic depression impact your daily life, and what
do you do to accommodate it?*

Alastair: Well, about a year ago I had a particularly severe manic episode where I was hospitalised for three months. The doctors changed my medication, and since then I've been quite flat – but not too flat. I think that's an important distinction to make, because in the past I've always been extremely flat after an episode of mania. The way I cope with it, at the moment, is by taking it day by day. I've become quite reclusive. I don't socialise too much. I hardly ring any of my friends anymore, which I used to do several times a week. And I don't go to the pub anymore, which I also used to do regularly. Plus, I spend a lot of time sleeping. But, having said that, I don't feel too bad.

The other major change is I've stopped smoking cannabis. Part of me thinks that cannabis can be a bit of a catalyst for mania, and that was one of the reasons I decided to give it up. Because of this, and the medication I'm on at the moment, I've managed to stay fairly stable.

Faye: That's quite revealing, isn't it, the connection you made between cannabis and mania.

Oh, absolutely. Cannabis is such a powerful drug and you get delusional on it. I used to love it, having smoked it pretty consistently since I was fourteen or fifteen. So it was a big thing to suddenly stop like that. But I'm glad I did. It was a decision I took for health reasons, and I plan to keep off of it from now on.

This applies to other drugs too. I've tried pretty much everything over the years. Cocaine, ecstasy, heroin – the whole spectrum. But my plan now is to have a drug-free life. Although, having said that, I drink a bottle of wine a night. Not more than that, but it is a bottle of wine nearly every evening. So I still have that vice.

Adam: But in the scheme of things you've made significant changes?

Yes, I have. And I think the reason I've made these changes was due to the last experience I had in the psychiatric unit. I was there for three months and I absolutely hated it. Consequently, I don't want to go back there. I don't want to ever be sectioned again. Prior to that, I hadn't been sectioned for about ten years, even though I had manic episodes all the time – one or two a year, in fact. This was the first time I'd been sectioned as a father, as I mentioned before. This had a huge impact on me and made me totally rethink the way I was living. Being away from my children, from my family. Being around people who were mentally ill. Locked up in a psychiatric unit for months on end. It was hell. So I don't want to go back there. I want to stay stable.

And, for the first time in ages, I don't have any desire

to be manic. I used to live for the manic episodes and look forward to them like you would a holiday or a good night out. Then when I was feeling that way, I'd think, God, I want this to last forever.

Adam: That sense of total freedom that comes with it.

Totally, totally. I would love being manic but, unfortunately, I'd then have to live with the consequences. Now, with hindsight, I can see how draining it all is, knowing what happens when I get so manic. The police showing up. The doctors showing up. Getting carted off to a psychiatric unit in a police van. None of these things are very pleasant but, for me, this is what happens.

Faye: Although I haven't had quite the same experiences with mania, I do know what it's like to be severely depressed in a psychiatric hospital. Most of my life has been spent trying to manage the effects of these episodes and to somehow prevent them from recurring. I think that's what all manic depressives try to do, whether consciously or unconsciously. No one would willingly subject themselves to those levels of distress without trying to do something about it. But it's never an easy task.

I think it's a fantastic decision to stop taking drugs, knowing how detrimental they are to your mental health. I never took drugs, apart from on the odd occasion when I was younger. But I do use alcohol to level out my mood swings, and have done for some time. I've also used fitness in the same way – running marathons and pushing myself physically to try to offset the terrible depressions. It's a constant balancing act. I'm not pretending there are any easy answers.

Adam: In my case, a big part of what I do on a daily basis to keep myself well is down to fear. I simply don't want to go back to that place I was at before. The psychiatrists, the hospitals, the utter chaos of it all. Whatever I can do to keep me from that is worth doing. When you go into the system manic and come out clinically depressed, it's like your brain's been through a meat grinder.

Alastair: You come out a zombie.

And it's the hardest thing in the world to recover from, to build yourself back up again. It takes huge reserves of strength and energy. There's a price you pay on the psychological as well as the physical level. I now value my health more than ever before – mental and physical.

Faye: Yes, and I think that's something that's often overlooked too, the toll it takes on your physical well being. I've run twenty two marathons, but the recovery from them was nothing compared to recovery from bouts of depression and mania. It takes everything from you, every last ounce of energy and willpower, and leaves you with nothing.

My daily life has definitely been affected. I've shied away from interacting with other people, mainly because I don't know how they'll deal with my fluctuating moods. I want to get back into mainstream life, to work and to study, but it's difficult, as I don't know how I'm going to be from one day to the next. Because of this, there's a real fear of exposing myself to the outside world.

Adam: How much has the illness affected your ability to work?

Well, I've recently tried to find voluntary work, but as I don't have references it's tough. Then you feel obligated to disclose all the details of your psychiatric history which is off-putting in itself. What would be ideal for me would be a period of stability, where I could feel confident enough to take something on. I don't want to be held back by my illness. I have hopes and dreams like anyone else and I want to fulfil them.

Alastair: I think the hardest thing of all to do is to adapt to ordinary life after all you've been through. When I went into hospital this last time, I was so high, so manic, it was incredible. The doctors and the staff were determined to bring me down, and the way they do that is by over-medicating. In the end, they were giving me 800 units of Clopixol a month, which is a depot injection, of which I was getting 200 units every week. I was also getting other medication on top of that in pill form, so God knows the level of medication I was on at that time.

But, as I said, the medication I'm on now has helped to keep me stable, so I'm grateful for that.

Faye: So you have a level of normality now, do you?

Yes, I do. Certainly when you compare it to how I was before.

One of the thing's that's changed in these last few months has been relations with my family. My father's been quite ill for some time, and because I've been feeling relatively stable I've been able to go over and help out. You know, do some of the duties a son should do. I can go shopping for them, or just look after my dad when my mum goes out. And part of it is because I feel so guilty because I've put them through so much. They've had to look after me and bail me out after so many awful episodes. I want to give them something back.

Adam: That's one of the things that gives me strength today. Knowing I can be of some use to my family, instead of continually going off the rails. It's a huge thing to be able to do what you're doing – helping your parents – to give something back. It raises your self-esteem.

'I don't want to be held
back by my illness.
I have hopes and
dreams like everyone
else and I want to
fulfil them.'

When I stopped drinking and taking drugs in 2004 it made a huge difference to my relations with my family, and everyone else around me. For the first time, I felt I had some control over my life, some balance. My moods were still volatile to a certain extent, but at least they weren't made worse by this added element.

On the subject of selfishness, I did read something the other day that made me think. Apparently, there's a psychiatric theory that people with bipolar have never got beyond the emotional stage of development where they think they're the centre of the universe. That would certainly explain some of the more extreme behavioural traits exhibited during mania.

Alastair: Oh absolutely! I'm sure there's a great deal of truth in that. It goes back to the superman theory we talked about earlier, doesn't it. Yes, you do think you're the centre of the universe, and everyone else's needs are secondary.

2. Has an awareness of your illness made you a better or, perhaps, stronger person?

Faye: That's quite hard for me to answer, really. Awareness of my condition has made me more conscious of what I need to do to be accepted by the 'mainstream' in society, but I still feel marginalised and left out. Maybe that's about my own perception, but that's how I feel. People expect so much of you, and you can't always live up to those expectations. Being depressed, or having any mental illness, isn't like having a cold where you have a few days off work and get over it. It takes huge emotional changes, and a certain amount of courage and energy to make that transition.

I think anyone who's lived with bipolar for a number of years comes out of it with an awareness of who they are, at least in terms of hopes and limitations. You get to know the things you can do and the things you can't, based on your previous experience. You get to know the triggers, the early-warning signs that might send you into another episode, and you try to avoid them at all costs.

As for being a stronger, or better person, I don't know. Because of what's happened to me, I am able to empathise more with others in the same position, but that's not the same thing. I certainly don't feel stronger, but that's a symptom of depression – it undermines everything and takes away your motivation to do anything.

Alastair: I don't think it's made me any better, or any stronger, really. Part of me is glad to be bipolar, purely because, had I not been, I would never have had these incredible experiences. It's like going to a place few people have been. You can't really relate to it unless you've been there. I think the only way people who aren't bipolar can get close to it is through drugs. By taking drugs, whether it be cocaine or ecstasy or whatever, you can reach similar heights of confidence and exuberance, but you can never come close to the experience of bipolar. I've said this before, if you could bottle mania and sell it you would be a millionaire.

Faye: Mania, without the consequences!

Exactly. Perhaps in a controlled, slow release form, over a few weeks or months. People would be queuing up to buy the stuff!

But, joking aside, you can't have a high without the low that comes with it. And with bipolar you go to the top of the mountain, so, consequently, you can expect to come crashing down to the bottom. It's one of those unfortunate consequences we talked about earlier.

Adam: I've often wondered about that Nietzsche saying 'That which doesn't kill us makes us stronger.' Martin Amis has his own amusing take on this, that goes something like, 'That which doesn't destroy us makes us weaker and kills us later.' My general view on this, kind of veers between the two, I suppose. Perhaps in some ways I am stronger, but it certainly doesn't feel like it sometimes. After all the things I've been through I should be dead. But, as Faye says, because of my experiences I can empathise with people who've been depressed, or hospitalised, because I know what it feels like. But that in itself doesn't make me stronger, or better in any way. All I do know is that I wouldn't want to go back there – either the troughs, or those incredible heights. I'd rather be somewhere in the middle.

Alastair: For the first time since I can remember, I don't want to go back there either. Even though the highs are so fantastic, the lows are such a nightmare, and I quite like being level at the moment. I like being a 'normal' human being.

Faye: Is that because of your last bout of mania?

Yes, it is really. I was hospitalised for three months, and that's the longest I've ever been in hospital due to mania. I was unbelievably high when they brought me in. Very delusional.

But generally I think of myself as a decent human being, and I wish everyone to be well, to have a good time and be happy. And I think I'm pretty honest. But whether any of that's down to my having a mental illness, I don't know. You'd have to be pretty insensitive to come away from all this without some level of empathy, wouldn't you?

Adam: In terms of self-acknowledgement, I think that's an important point to qualify. I'm more comfortable with myself now than at any time in the past, although I have my moments, I can assure you. But compared to how I used to be, my life today is a vast improvement. I used to feel I was on a knife-edge all the time, that I could go either way. Consequently, I was using things to self-medicate and control the way I was feeling, without much success. Life seemed to get harder. Now I don't have that same level of desperation.

Faye: That's what I'm looking for, really. That stability. That way of coping without using things I know aren't good for me. Having bipolar has been such a disruption in my life that I feel I've not been able to live up to my true potential. And this isn't a cop-out, or self-pity or anything, but more an observation on how it's been for me over the years.

Ideally, I'd like to get on and do things, like finish the novel I started, and enrol in further education. Show people that mental illness isn't an end but a different way of seeing.

Alastair: I like that. *A different way of seeing*. Because, ultimately, that's what it's all about, isn't it. The way you see yourself. Your own perceptions. As I said before, I don't have any grand motivations that drag me out of bed in the morning, so having ambitions or desires doesn't really apply. I don't know how much that has to do with the medication I'm on, which does make me feel quite tired and lazy most of the time. But I'm not too depressed. I've got my family, I've got two kids. So I've got a lot to be grateful for.

Adam: And that's a huge thing isn't it, the family unit?

Absolutely, I think it is. That's why I was shocked to get sectioned this time. After the last time, I thought, right that's it, I've got children now, I'm not going to be selfish and put myself in that position again. But that's what happened, and I don't want it to happen again.

3. What do you do to stay well?

Alastair: At the moment, I take a depot injection of Clopixol every two weeks. Also, when I came out of hospital, I was very flat, very down, and they put me on a course of antidepressants as well. I've found that they've helped with my mood. I'm not as anxious or panicky. I'm not as depressed or unhappy as I was. I feel more normal than I've ever felt, certainly than I've felt for a number of years.

As I said earlier, I try to take it day by day. I try not to look too far into the future, or I'll get anxious about some appointment in a week's time. Sometimes, if I find I'm getting too fixated on some future event, I'll say to myself, hey, you'll cope with it, just take it day by day and see how tomorrow is. And, as a coping strategy, I'd say it works well for me. Otherwise you're bringing the future to the present, and that's not a good thing to do.

Faye: Being a scientist, and having a great belief in research and medicine, I don't have much faith in any treatments outside of that sphere. I suppose that makes me a sceptic, although I'm willing to admit some of these things may be of benefit to other people. It's just that I'm not one of them. Apart from the running, and my writing, I don't do anything you might describe as 'therapeutic'. I see my mental illness as a chemical imbalance that can be corrected largely through medication, and with ongoing assessment from a medical team.

But, in saying that, I do believe in the importance of counselling, or therapy of some sort. I've been down that road myself before, and continue to do so, in the hope that, in time, it will help me. Many of my issues are deep rooted and go back a long way, so consequently need a lot of working on. But I do have a determination to succeed. I know I'll never stop trying.

Alastair: Could you ever see yourself medication free?

I don't know. That would largely depend on my moods and whether or not I could remain stable for any length of time without medication. At the moment I can't see it, but it's certainly something I'd like to think I could achieve in the future. But like I said, I'm a scientist. Unless something changed radically in my mental state I'd have to keep on relying on the doctors and the drug companies to keep me stable.

Adam: I was always looking for a miracle cure when my illness was at its height. I went through a stage of seeking out mediums and faith healers, hypnotists and astrologers. Anyone I thought would be able to wave some magic wand and pronounce me cured in one sitting. I soon realised this was hopelessly unrealistic and accepted there was no magic cure.

The answer, for me, lay in making certain lifestyle changes and, when I made these, I started to see significant improvements in all areas. Drugs and alcohol are a no-no for me now. I can look back on the impact they made on my illness with a clarity now that I didn't have back then. However volatile my mental state may have been at any one time, drinking or taking drugs made it much worse. Some of the things I did, and certain experiences I had under the influence of alcohol, in particular, have convinced me that I can never safely drink again. The same goes for drugs. Apart from the street drugs I took sporadically, I also developed a reliance on benzodiazepines, which continued after I'd stopped drinking. One mental health nurse pointed out, quite rightly, that this was simply replacing one addiction with another, and eventually I stopped these also.

I also try to maintain a certain level of fitness, to counteract any downswings in my mood. Although I don't do as much now as I used to, I still keep up a regime of swimming and cycling. I've also come to enjoy walking, which is a surprise, as I used to find it totally boring when I was younger. I also do a brief T'ai Chi warm-up routine most mornings, which helps centre the mind and relaxes the body. I love the slow, calming movements, and the sense of peace it can instil, however transient this may be in the course of a busy day.

But, having said all that, I'm still aware of the triggers. I don't want to put myself in situations that might send me one way or another. It's a kind of balancing act, really. But I think, like anything else, you get better as you practise it.

Alastair: Although I'm experiencing quite a stable period at the moment, I have to say that I don't tend to look forward to things particularly. I don't get excited about things. I mean, my partner's getting excited about us going on holiday. Now I haven't been abroad for ten years, but to be honest I don't want to go. I don't want to do anything, really. There's this underlying state of flatness that affects everything. With my parents I will do things because I feel I have to, that it's my duty. But on the whole, I don't want to do a thing. I just want to have life as easy and as stress free as possible, and also as idle as possible.

Adam: Well you've always been brutally honest about that!

Yes, I have, and I see no reason not to be. This is my reality, my life, and the things I have to go through on a daily basis. Other people's experience might be different, and that's okay, but this is how it feels for me.

Faye: There is a theory out there that all medication is bad for you, that we should all be drug free for the good of our health. But when you look at psychiatric drugs, they are designed specifically with one purpose, and that's to reduce the symptoms or the severity of mental illness. Lithium, for instance, is a natural salt, and although it can be toxic if the dose is too high, it has proved to be effective in controlling bipolar.

Alastair: So it's pretty much all medication for you?

To a certain extent, yes. I don't want to dismiss other treatments outright, but I am sceptical. I do like hearing other bipolars talking about their experiences, and that's been one of the purposes of this book. The sharing of knowledge. Giving hope to other sufferers out there.

Adam: Well I'm going to play devil's advocate here and say that, in my mind, the best possible scenario for anyone, whether they have a mental illness or not, is to live drug free. That's the best option, without a doubt. Some of these chemicals are incredibly powerful and have all kinds of side effects that can impact negatively on your general health.

But, having said that, I accept that certain drugs, like the ones we've mentioned, have a part to play in stabilising mental illness. I've been on lithium for the best part of ten years now, and it's helped keep me on an even keel. When I tried to come off of it a few years ago, my mood changed very quickly. I started to stay up writing through the night, and had all these grandiose ideas I'd then phone people and tell them about. Luckily, I had enough insight to recognise things weren't right and made an appointment to see the doctor. She recommended I go back on the lithium right away, which I did.

Alastair: The proof is in the pudding, as they say. When I was brought into hospital the last time I was so manic, but then they gave me this depot injection and it brought me right down. Now they've reduced the dose to an acceptable level so I don't feel too flat and I feel okay. I would love some sort of guarantee that I could stay like this indefinitely, but that's not possible. All I can do is focus on what's keeping me well at the moment and build on that.

Faye: Is it all about medication for you, then?

Not entirely, but I certainly believe it's been instrumental in keeping me stable. My Community Psychiatric Nurse told me I was classic bipolar, and he was referring to the delusions, the belief that I was some kind of deity, or had special powers. But I don't have those delusions anymore. They're gone. And if that's down to the medication I'm on, then so be it.

But I can understand people who want to come off the medication. After a while you get to the stage where you think, hey, I feel totally normal now, I can behave like a normal human being, I can have conversations and not freak anyone out. Your next thought is, God, do I need the medication at all? Maybe I'm totally cured, totally fine. Then, like Adam says, you come off the medication and the mood swings return. You're back where you started.

I think the way to look at it, is that bipolar is an illness, like diabetes, which I also have. So I need the medication to control it, just as I need insulin.

Adam: What about alternative treatments?

Well, I did go and see a spiritual healer years ago, at the behest of my mother, who thought it might help me in some way. This was probably ten or so years ago, after my friend in London had killed himself. My parents had always believed that this particular incident had been the catalyst for my becoming bipolar. Now I don't know if that's the case or not. Part of me thinks it might have been when I was living in America, in Los Angeles, smoking cannabis every day. I was smoking this really strong skunk, which is extremely powerful, so perhaps it could have been that.

At the moment, I'm just relieved I'm not in the grip of the illness, whether depressed or manic, and that I'm able to function, to a degree, without that level of disruption in my life. I think we're all looking for some form of stability, don't you?

Adam: When you've experienced manic depression at its height, you know how devastating it can be to you and everyone around you. Stability doesn't figure highly in your day to day living. But yes, certainly for me, having some level of control or normality is crucial. Awareness is the key. Knowing what the triggers are, and which areas to avoid. Every little thing I can do to keep myself well is worth it in the long run.

Faye: I'm still hopeful for the future, in that I can achieve the things I want to achieve and not be held back in any way. It's finding the strength, the resilience to go on, after so many setbacks and disappointments. You have to believe that it's worthwhile.

Chris's View

As previously stated, recovery is not a new concept within mental health. In recent times, it has come to the fore of service development and continues to shape the practice of all those involved with supporting the service user and their family. The problems of recovery and personal identity for those faced with mental health issues is an ongoing process, often requiring a change in attitudes and values. The goal for each individual is to live a productive and meaningful life, in spite of the illness, and to find ways to achieve this.

Four elements are:

- » Hope
- » Identity
- » Meaning
- » Personal responsibility

What is clear from the evidence and the stories shared by Faye, Alastair and Adam is the individual nature of recovery. You can read contrasting views from all three, as they discuss how they understand their shared illness, how they live with the symptoms, and how they believe it is treated.

Recovery has been described as a journey. We are fortunate to have three shared experiences of the illness in which to identify with.

Therefore, recovery is not just about having access to health services, but rather a personal process of modifying attitudes and feelings. By developing values, skills, aims and identity, each client works towards a better future. Recovery is empowerment. Each person develops a path towards their recovery.

Recovery also incorporates the concept of empowerment. This will result in the person contributing positively and taking an active role in the networks around them.

Perhaps, at this stage, it might be helpful to summarise some of the information given throughout this book. These are not intended as 'commandments', only as tips and advice drawn from both my experience as a healthcare professional, and the combined experience of Adam, Faye and Alastair in living with bipolar disorder.

Do speak to your family about what is happening.

» Seek professional help
» Avoid illicit drugs
» Have confidence in your abilities (remember past achievements)
» Accept that you are having problems (they need not last forever)
» Plan for recovery
» Persevere with medication
» Discuss medication with your mental health team
» Read about bipolar disorder
» Ask questions
» Keep a record of appointments and get someone else to do the same
» Be mindful how much alcohol you drink
» Engage in your treatment – it works!
» Plan ahead – what are the consequences of your choices?
» Be cautious of any 'alternative' treatments and discuss first with your doctor
» Think about your routine: sleep, diet and exercise matter!
» Join a support group for those with bipolar disorder
» Suggest a family member does the same

» See being depressed or manic as part of an illness and seek treatment for it

» Remember – if you could 'pull yourself together' you would

» Recovery is important and involves doing something each day

» Set goals, no matter how small

» Learn about your own early warning signs and develop a plan to cope with them

Advice and tips for family and friends

» Stay positive (never give up hope)

» Have faith in the person's abilities to cope (this will help build their self-esteem)

» Accept their limitations

» Provide practical support

» Tackle any problems at home which may be contributing to increased stress

» Seek out help/advice/support from: friends and family, job centre, Relate, medical centres and your own GP

» Encourage person to be active

» Help design a plan for recovery

» Avoid blaming

» Try not to be over-protective

» Avoid phrases like, 'pull yourself together'

» Emphasise the fact that each person is living their life, not just coping. Enjoy your life!

Appendix

Recovery in Action

Learning self-determination and responsibility is another way of building confidence. This way, you act as a role model, and teach others about living with the illness. By involving the support system of family and friends, you know when to hand over temporary responsibility, accepting that recovery is an ongoing process.

Self-management means making use of services without being taken over by professionals. Health care practitioners can be there by invitation only. Working with such services ensures that the 'them and us' barriers are removed and a better partnership develops.

Getting the right balance between work, socialising, and being alone is also extremely important. Learn to pace yourself and set personal boundaries. See recovery as taking control, and use this control as a strength for the times ahead. You are the 'director' in the process of recovery, and have an untapped capacity to change and grow.

Practising self-acceptance can be hugely beneficial. You may wish to explore spiritual avenues to help with this, or take up some form of meditation. Understand that while medication helps you manage your illness, *you* manage *your* life. Many people make a full recovery.

The cornerstone of recovery is Self:

> » Self-confidence
> » Self-esteem
> » Self-awareness
> » Self-acceptance

Accept that many things can aid recovery, but no one thing helps everyone. By seeking your own answers, and not listening to negative people, you experience growth and positive change. Adopt a positive attitude. Have a vision for the future that includes meaningful relationships, goals and ambitions. Above all, face whatever has happened in the past and be hopeful.

While recording your first weeks' activities, pay attention to two variables: Pleasure and Mastery. Has the activity you've written down provided you with any pleasure? If so, write a P in the box and rate the pleasurable activity on a scale from 1 (minimal pleasure) to 10 (extreme pleasure).

Mastery activities are those in which you take care of yourself or others.

Identifying and rating Pleasure and Mastery activities is very important, and may help you see how life has gotten out of balance; perhaps the things you formerly enjoyed no longer give you any pleasure.

Pleasure ratings also give you information about the activities you still enjoy, and which ones offer the best boost to your mood. Conversely, rating Mastery activities helps you find a balance, to see when you're doing things just to cope. Remember, you may not be as efficient or effective as you were before becoming depressed, but the things you do are real achievements. Keeping a chart will help you to see this.

Try not to underestimate yourself and what you might achieve, or how difficult it is to be productive during a bout of depression. Increasing both pleasurable and mastery activities during your week is a good way of making progress.

Pleasure Activities might include:

> » visiting friends/family
> » phone calls to friends/family
> » movies/plays/TV
> » exercise
> » sports activities
> » internet
> » computer games,
> » music
> » planning a holiday

Many of the things of the things you've enjoyed in the past might seem lacking in interest now. Depression turns the things you once looked forward to into a burden. But these feelings will pass as you begin to recover. Scheduling pleasurable activities into your week will make you feel better, even if those same activities seem uninteresting right now.

There may be activities you haven't recorded because you consider them insignificant. When you're depressed *everything* is of significance, no matter how small you think it is.

Mastery activities might include:

- » Food shopping
- » Ironing
- » Paying bills
- » Having a bath
- » Washing your clothes
- » Driving
- » Going to work
- » Fixing something
- » Making the bed
- » Cooking
- » Washing up
- » Walking the dog
- » Cleaning house/car
- » Exercise
- » Picking up the kids from school

By recording what you do, you can see if you are doing too much or not enough. (Perhaps you are avoiding certain things e.g. going out or paying bills). Try not to avoid those things you don't like!

By planning your activities you can do things that make you feel positive/good about yourself. Doing nothing often makes you feel worse. Try something on the list and evaluate what happens. How you feel may change as you go through the activity.

As the week passes, record your scores and compare them to the anticipated ones. As depression can lead you to be more pessimistic in your outlook, the scores you anticipate will probably be far lower than the actual experience.

A sense of achievement can be derived from accomplishing the tasks you set for yourself. By 'beating depression' you help defeat the thinking which would have prevented you from attempting the task in the first place.

I have done this exercise with service users countless times and the results are always illuminating. People often underestimate how much they are actually doing (getting the kids to school, cooking a family meal etc). Conversely, if a persons' schedule is full of 'Pleasure' activities only, there is a high probability they are either going on holiday, or their mood is elevated.

Chris Kelly

Further Reading

A wealth of information is now available on bipolar disorder – sometimes you may feel there is too much. The internet is one source, but be wary of misinformation, or simply information that is hard to apply to your own experience. Finding comprehensive and effective self-help literature can help you or your family to manage the range of difficulties that are part of bipolar disorder.

We hope the following prove useful to you:

An Unquiet Mind - Kay Redfield Jamison Random House 1997

Touched with Fire: Manic Depressive Illness and the Artistic Temperment - Kay Redfield Jamison 1996 - New York: Free Press

Cognitive Therapy for Bipolar Disorder: A Therapist's Guide to Concepts, Methods and Practice - 2010 - Dominic Lam. Wiley Series.

A Brilliant Madness: Living with Manic-Depressive Illness - Patty Duke and Gloria Hochman Bantam Books 1992

Fear Strikes Out: The Jim Piersall Story - Jim Piersall and Al Hirshberg, Little, Brown and Co. 1955

Mind Power - James Borg

Surviving Manic Depression: A Manual on Bipolar Disorder for Patients, Families and Providers - E. Fuller Torrey, M.D. and Michael B. Knable, D.O. Basic Books 2000

Overcoming Depression: A self- help guide using Cognitive Behavioural Techniques - Paul Gilbert 2009 - Constable and Robinson Ltd

Depression - Dr. Paul Hauck

Guidelines on Bipolar Disorder and other Mental Health problems:

http://www.psychguides.com/guides/living-with-bipolar-disorder/

http://www.moodswings.org.uk

Overcoming Mood Swings - Jan Scott 2010 Constable and Robinson Ltd

Overcoming Sleep Problems - Colin Epsie 2006 Constable and Robinson Ltd

Psychiatric Drugs Explained - 2004 - David Healey, Churchill Livingstone

http://www.nhs.uk/Conditions/Bipolar-disorder/Pages/Introduction.aspx

http://www.nhs.uk/conditions/social-care-and-support-guide/Pages/what-is-social-care.aspx

Leaflets

Making sense of lithium and other mood stabilisers MIND, 2011

The management of bipolar disorder in adults, children and adolescents, in primary and secondary care Nice, 2006

Bipolar UK - www.bipolaruk.org.uk

MDF Bipolar Organisation - www.mdf.org.uk

Mind - www.mind.org.uk

Pendulum Resources - www.pendulum.org

SANE UK - www.sane.org.uk

Royal College of Psychiatrists - www.rcpsych.ac.uk

United States

Depression and bipolar support alliance - www.dbsalliance.org

International Bipolar Foundation (IBPF) - www.internationalbipolarfoundation.org

International Society for Bipolar disorders - www.isbd.org

Mental Health America - www.nmha.org

National Alliance on Mental Illness (NAMI) - www.nami.org

National Mental Health Information Centre (NMHIC) - www.mentalhealth.samhsa.gov

Bipolarbrain - www.bipolarbrain.com

Summary

In writing an account of bipolar disorder from the sufferer's point of view, there is always the danger that much of the content will be seen as anecdotal, and not contain enough 'facts' for the keen researcher. *Surfing the Edge* is an attempt to bring the day to day realities of living with the illness to the attention of the reader, and to reveal some of the difficulties that occur as a result. One of the major problems is compliance with medication. As the illness causes extreme fluctuations in mood, it is often difficult to maintain long periods of stability.

Taking medication is often seen as one more restriction, something else to undermine the patient's individuality and restrict freedom. But the ravages of the illness are considerable and, in themselves, form a persuasive argument in favour of compliance. Medication may not be the most desirable option, but in the case of severe mania and depression, it is the most effective in bringing the symptoms under control.

Lifestyle changes may well be the key to a more stable future. Reduction or elimination of drugs and alcohol is a start. So called recreational drugs can play havoc with moods and can trigger an episode of mania or depression. Stimulants such as cocaine and amphetamines mimic the symptoms of mania and produce, among other things, agitation, sleep loss and paranoia. Alcohol reduces inhibitions, interferes with sleep patterns and causes depression

The use of drugs and/or alcohol should be seen as a significant factor in the recurrence of the illness, and, therefore, something to be avoided.

Support networks play a vital role in maintaining the health and well-being of the individual. There are many organisations and self-help groups that have been set up to help which you can find online, or by visiting your local library. These organisations provide free support and information and, in some cases, are run by bipolar sufferers themselves. For a selection of these, see the reference section at the back of this book.

In spite of the severity of the illness, there are many safeguards that can be put in place that can either reduce or prevent symptoms from returning. Lifestyle changes, compliance with medication, and an understanding of the triggers can all help to make bipolar disorder more manageable and enhance the quality of life for those affected.

CBT is also recommended. As the mind is the most powerful tool in your arsenal, it makes sense to use it to maximise your recovery. There are many techniques you can learn that will help you deal with unwanted thoughts and recognise negative thinking patterns. The more positive changes you can make, the greater the chances of staying stable and living life to the best of your ability.

Adam Dickson